thea porter

V&A Publishing

thea porter

Laura McLaws Helms and Venetia Porter

In memory of Thea Porter (1927–2000)

First published by V&A Publishing, 2015
Victoria and Albert Museum
South Kensington
London SW7 2RL
www.vandapublishing.com

Distributed in North America by Abrams,
an imprint of ABRAMS

Hardback edition
ISBN 978 1 85177 826 3

Library of Congress Control Number 2014951840

10 9 8 7 6 5 4 3 2 1
2019 2018 2017 2016 2015

A catalogue record for this book is available
from the British Library.

Design Myfanwy Vernon-Hunt for This Side
Copy-editor Rebeka Cohen
Index Hilary Bird

New photography by the V&A Photographic Studio

Printed in Hong Kong

Front cover Anne Schaufuss in an antique *ikat* tunic.
Photograph by Clive Arrowsmith (see p.89).

Back cover Thea Porter outside her shop on Greek Street.

Page 2 Thea's assistants Claudia Bruce and Bruno Mossa.
The fabrics for the background and Claudia's *abaya* are by
Sandra Munro. Photograph by Aubrey Powell, 1970.

Page 8 Sandra Munro's 1970 textile design was based
Samawa carpets (detail; see p.59).

Page 62 Chiffon patchwork pattern by Sandra Munro
(detail; see p.78).

Page 102 Lily print on satin by Janet Taylor (detail;
see p.82).

Page 114 White chiffon dress with Indian-style gold
sequin embroidery (detail; see p.118).

Page 124 Silk georgette gown (detail; see page 129).

Page 136 Peacock print by Sandra Munro, inspired
by Aubrey Beardsley (detail; see p.78).

Page 150 Drawing of Thea Porter by Ffolks. Originally
accompanied an article by David Taylor in *Punch*.
11 December 1974.

Contents

'Whatever else clothes may be about, I believe they must add to the enjoyment of life. A dress is a failure unless it gives a woman added confidence. She must put it on, feel great, and then forget that she is wearing it and get on with her life.'

Thea Porter, **Scrapbook**

For nearly two decades, from 1966, Thea Porter created clothes made from sumptuous fabrics that drew much of their inspiration from an exotic view of the Middle East. Often combining richly patterned silks with antique fabrics, her clothes were treasured by those who owned them. Dressing such music and film stars as Pink Floyd, Crystal Gayle, Elizabeth Taylor and Barbra Streisand, while featuring in fashion magazines all over the world, Thea was a key member of an innovative group of British designers which included Ossie Clark, Zandra Rhodes and Jean Muir. During her lifetime she won huge acclaim, and her place in the history of British Fashion was recognized by the award of Designer of the Year in 1972. Despite being included in landmark exhibitions on twentieth-century fashion such as the Victoria and Albert Museum's *Cutting Edge: Fifty Years of Fashion* (1997), *Orientalism: Visions of the East in Western Dress* at the Metropolitan Museum of Art (1994) and most recently *Hippie Chic* at the Boston Museum of Fine Arts (2013), however, her name was gradually forgotten, until a recent resurgence of interest in vintage fashion attracted attention from contemporary celebrities.[1]

This is the first publication to consider Thea's work in detail, to look at the sources of her inspiration, and to place that achievement at the heart of British Fashion of the second half of the twentieth century. It demonstrates how her ambition to create clothes that were intrinsically beautiful, and that would last, is now appreciated by new devotees who continue to seek out her designs: Kate Moss, Julia Roberts, Nicole Richie, Ashley and Mary-Kate Olsen – the appeal of a unique and original Thea Porter dress endures today among some of the most fashionable women in the public eye.

This book accompanies an exhibition at the Fashion and Textile Museum in London.[2] It begins with Thea's family history and upbringing in Syria, her years as a student in London after the Second World War, and her life in the cosmopolitan city of Beirut during the 1950s and 1960s.[3] Further chapters discuss Thea as dress designer, following the trajectories of the business she set up, starting with the iconic Greek Street shop in Soho, and charting the dramatic rise of interest in her clothes in America and the opening of her shop in Paris. This, the body of the book, reflects the painstaking work of fashion historian Laura McLaws Helms, who as a student fell in love with Thea Porter clothes and set about researching the history of her business.[4] Laura's starting point was an archive donated to the V&A that comprises press cuttings, patterns and detailed documents relating to the business. It also includes an unpublished memoir by Thea that she entitled 'Thea Porter's Scrapbook' and which she began writing before being affected by Alzheimer's disease in the mid-1990s. Laura has found and interviewed many of Thea's customers and friends, and the people who had worked for her over many years, designing fabrics, making the dresses or running the shops. One of these was Louise Fennell, and it was her loyalty to Thea that created the impetus for both the exhibition and book. I am grateful to her, and to Saleh Barakat, who supported the publication, which has enabled us to turn the dream of reviving the memory of Thea Porter into reality.

Thea Porter's ambition was to create dresses 'beyond trend and tat, that thirty years from today will still be beautiful'.[5] All of us involved in the book and the exhibition are delighted that a new generation is once again wearing the dresses she produced, and that the magic of Thea's designs has proved to be both compelling and timeless.

Venetia Porter

Thea Porter was born Dorothea Noelle Naomi Sigel in Jerusalem in 1927 and grew up in Syria. She was one of three children: Barbara the eldest was born in 1924, and Patrick the youngest, in 1930. Their father Morris was also born in Jerusalem, in 1896; his family were Russian Jews, by the name of Yevilovitch, who had migrated to Palestine in the 1880s. Originally from a rabbinical family, Morris's father left for America in about 1900, to obtain funds, it was said, for the nascent migrant Jewish community. But he never returned, starting a new family in America instead.

Morris and his brother Henry remained in Jerusalem and were brought up by their grandmother, their mother having died giving birth to Morris. As a young man, Morris was apprenticed to a printer, who sent him to Antwerp and from there he moved on to London in 1912 where he was joined by his brother Henry. Living in the East End, Morris joined the Jewish Mission, which aimed to convert Jews to Christianity.[1] As a convert from Palestine, able to speak both Arabic and Hebrew, he was the ideal candidate to work in the Anglican mission in Jerusalem, where he was then sent.

Thea's mother Reine Marie Attal (known as Renée) was one of about 12 children born in Tunisia to Eric, a Tunisian Jew working for the French administration. Her mother's family name was Bigiave, a family of Italian–Jewish origin who at some stage may have converted to Catholicism. Three of Renée's brothers were killed in the First World War, and she came to England in 1916 intending to become a doctor, but instead trained to be a midwife.[2]

Morris and Renée must have met in London at about this time and together they travelled to Jerusalem where they were married in 1922 (p.11). Morris was returning to the city he had left as a Jew, knowing that his family would cut him out of their lives for that act of apostasy, but it was not something he ever spoke of. He ran the Anglican mission school in Jerusalem and Renée used her skills as a midwife. In the late 1920s, Morris came under the influence of the Irish Presbyterians, and travelled to Belfast to study Theology at the

damascus & beirut

Venetia Porter & Laura McLaws Helms

'An exotic childhood is an incalculable asset for a designer or indeed any sort of artist. Mine was certainly exotic and also idyllic.'

Presbyterian College between 1929 and 1930, which would prepare him for the work he was to do in Syria. He and Renée then went to Damascus for a probationary period and, following his official ordination in Belfast in 1933, they returned to Syria where they were to remain until 1950.[3]

Syria in 1931 was under the French Mandate, which had been established in 1920.[4] By 1936 the French had agreed to independence, but remained there – the Nationalist government having conceded to French military and economic dominance. The Second World War was approaching and, in 1940, Syria came under the control of the Axis dominated Vichy government following the occupation of France by Germany. In 1941, Syria was occupied by British troops and those of the Free French and, a year after the end of the war, the French finally left. The following year, 1947, the Arab Ba'th party was founded and the history of Syria over the following decades was characterized by complicated political manoeuvres involving military coups, unsuccessful alliances with neighbours Egypt and Iraq, and the rise of Hafiz al-Asad, an Alawi officer who was to take power in Syria in 1970.[5]

Early life

It is against this background that the Sigel family lived their lives. Thea describes how in the mid to late 1930s: 'the Syrians were constantly rioting against the French ... gangs of boys would stone the passing trams ... the space beneath our balcony often packed with screaming men.' The French troops would restore the peace 'with black Senegalese troops whose rolling eyes and fearsome knives struck fear into the Damascenes.'[6] Amid this political unrest, Thea remembered her father, who was running a number of schools in Damascus by then, as being more concerned with education than with trying to convert people. He gave his sermons in Arabic and 'spent most of his time patching up quarrels between his parishioners – they were a disputatious lot; getting people out of jail; giving small sums of money and old clothes to down- and-outs ... running a night school where sweaty boys lifted weights and played ping-pong; and generally trying to do good.'[7]

Thea describes her mother as 'a small energetic Frenchwoman ... frequently out delivering babies or looking after the sick.'[8] But there was

Above, left to right
Wedding of Morris and Renée in Jerusalem, 11 October 1922. Photograph by Khalil Raad.

The Rev. Morris Sigel (later Seale), his wife Renée and children Barbara, Patrick and Thea. Belfast, about 1933. Photograph by Charles H. Halliday.

Thea aged six wearing her favourite dress with puffed sleeves. Damascus, 3 July 1934.

another side to Renée, which Thea describes as an 'unsatisfied longing for luxury. She was a hoarder of pretty bits and pieces. The sheets in her linen cupboard were interspersed with Damascus brocade, silver threaded silks, French soaps, bottles and stockings. She had two treasured velvet dresses, one ruby-red with six-sided silver buttons traveling up the cuff, the other shimmering black.'[9] Most importantly she knew her way around the wonderful covered bazar known as *Suq al-Hamidieh* in Damascus: 'trailing after her I learnt about the spices and condiments, about the bewildering variety of sweetmeats ... about ice cream scented with mastic and pistachios ... but also about fabrics and trimmings and buttons, and lace; about gold, bangles and precious stones; about perfumes, scents and essential oils.'[10] Thea's earliest memory of her own clothes at this time was of a dress (*above*) made from a length of periwinkle blue silk given by one of the missionaries: 'it had short puffed sleeves, smocked in pink above the elbow ... it was the most beautiful thing I had ever owned and I like to think it started me on my career.'[11]

Bloudan – an idyll

The village of Bloudan was where the family spent their summers (p.12). High up in the mountains above Damascus, 'its donkey trails leading to luxuriant orchards, and above all air as crisp as the Alps and a night sky so bright one could read by it.'[12] They had a huge house with a church within the enormous grounds; there were fruit, walnut and almond trees and a tree house. 'We would make drinks from rose petals ... or just sit on little stools in the stream running though the garden, in the shade of the poplar trees.'[13]

Left, from top The Presbyterian mission summer house in Bloudan where Thea spent her childhood. Bloudan, Syria, 1930s.

A walk in the hills around the family home in Bloudan. Thea and her mother in the foreground. Bloudan, Syria, early 1930s.

Thea in the garden of the family summer house. Bloudan, Syria, mid-1940s.

As her brother Patrick was to write some years later, 'Thea was smitten with Alzheimer's disease in her last years and lost not just the power of speech, and all recollection of her career, even the way to her mouth with a spoon. Yet, one day, walking silently in the park, collecting little bouquets of dead leaves, she suddenly uttered the single word: "Bloudan".'[14]

England

The end of the war in 1945 put a stop to this idyll, and both Thea and Patrick were sent to boarding schools in England: Thea, now 18, to Fernhill Manor in Hampshire from 1946 to 1947,[15] to prepare her for the Higher School Certificate that she needed to get into university, and Patrick to Monkton Combe. A collection of some 50 letters (*overleaf*) from Thea to her parents survive from the years 1946 to 1949 while she was at Fernhill, and later at Royal Holloway College. These letters, sometimes written weekly, are vivacious and give an evocative picture of post-war England, complete with tales of coupons, shortages and electricity cuts. They are full of news of her friends and her studies; she learns the violin, decides she wants to be a journalist. She refers frequently to clothes – or, mostly, a lack of them.

Clothes were in short supply due to rationing, and Thea was on a meagre allowance, so her mother would send her parcels with garments she had made for her daughter. In February 1947, Thea wrote: 'you are an angel for making me an evening jumper with sequins!'[16] In March, she sends her mother her foot measurements: it was easier to get shoes in Damascus than in ration-stricken London.[17] Later she writes, 'Mummy please when next you send me a pair of stockings (how hopeful!) don't send me silk, the two pairs I had were ruined irretrievably the 1st time I wore them.'[18]

Her mother would send her fabric expecting her to make her own clothes, but Thea was often in despair: in May 1947 she explained that 'the parcel June is bringing sounds smashing but I think you rate my dress making skills too high, I don't know what the skirt will look like when I will have made it.'[19] In a letter dated 8 June, she was ecstatic: 'I want to thank you not only for the things which are lovely, but, especially for all the love & care behind it ... that marvellous dressing gown and the slippers ... Everyone is very jealous of me and the two lovely frocks, they fit perfectly ... and last of all the dream jumper. I really went wild over it and I am waiting for my brown silk skirt to arrive to try it on.'[20] As the end of 1947 approached, Thea noted that Mrs Shewell-Cooper (her guardian) had arranged for them to go to a 'posh' place for Christmas and was asked if she had anything that could be made up. Thea wrote (*see below*): 'So I thought of a lovely splodgy dress length I have ... I have just taken it to along to the dress-maker along with a pattern that I drew. It should be quite sweet with a sort of 'tulip' skirt. It looks foul in the sketch I am afraid.'[21]

Below Undated letter from Thea to her parents, including a sketch of a tulip skirt she designed. Probably Autumn 1947.

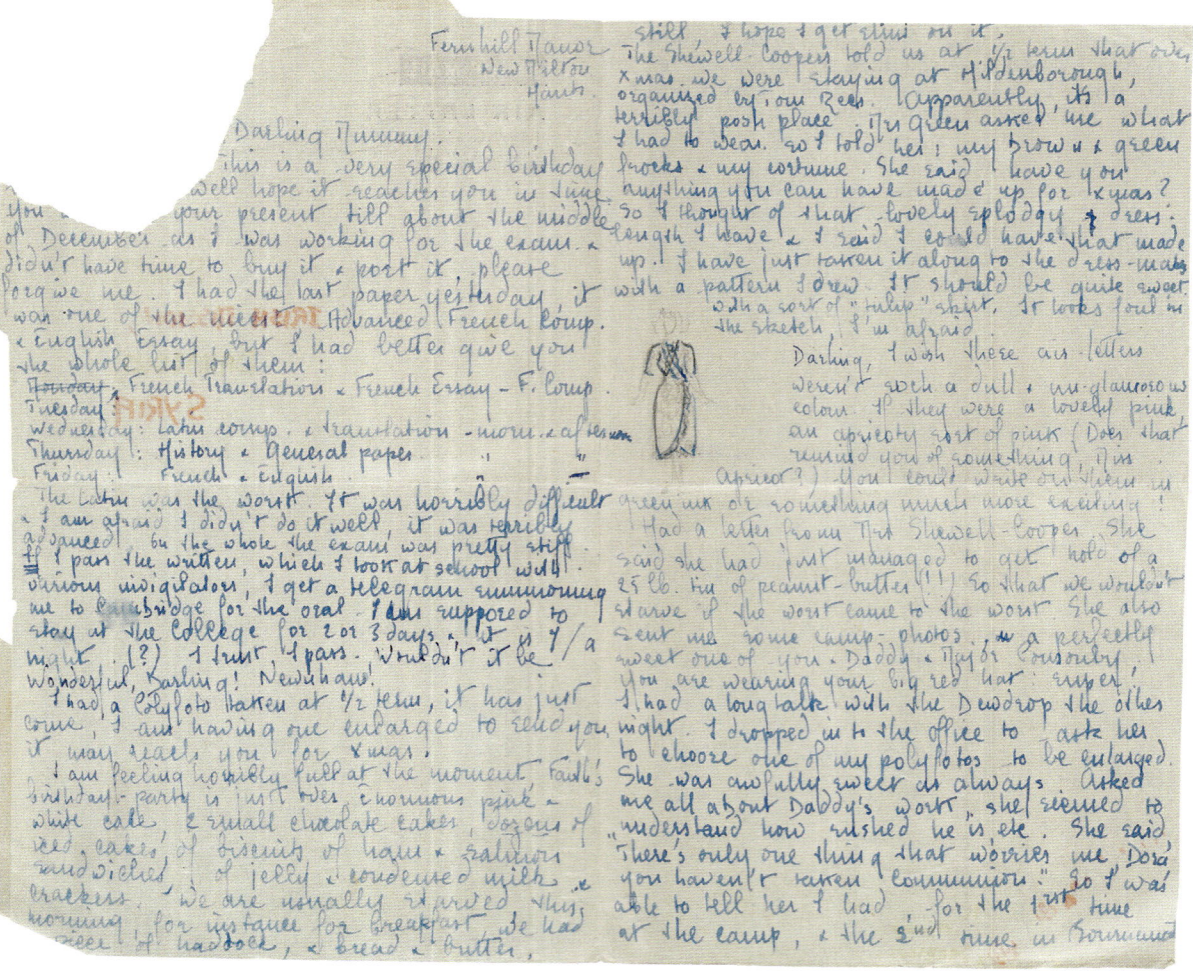

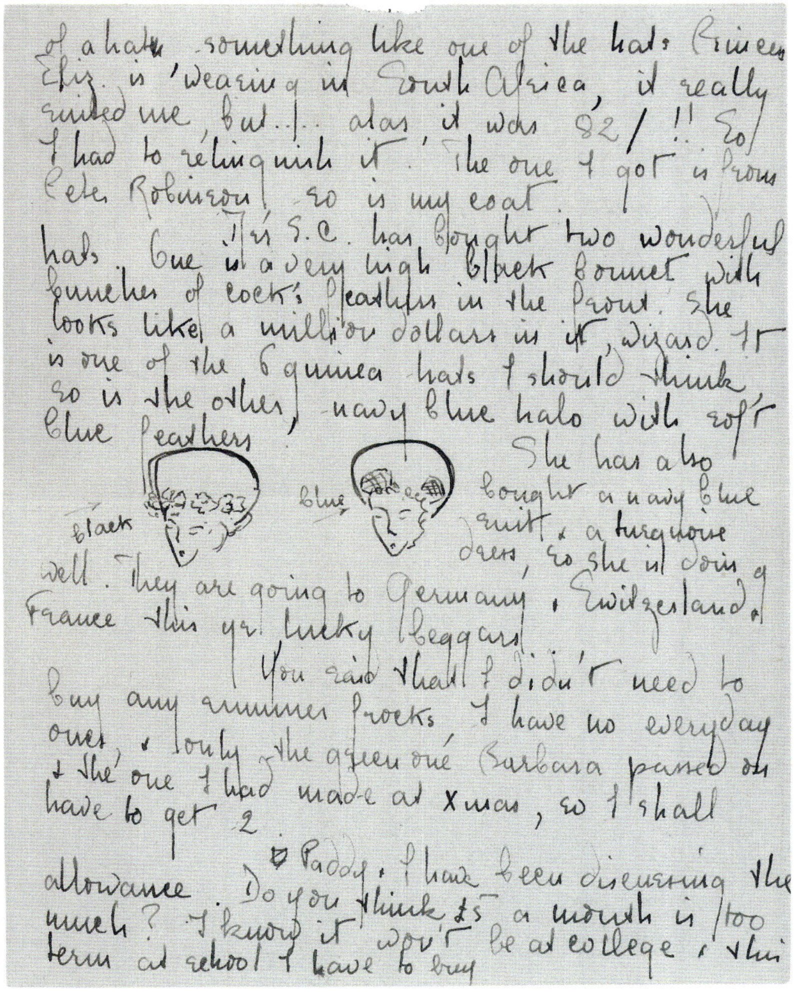

of a hat, something like one of the hats Princess Eliz. is wearing in South Africa, it really suited me, but... alas, it was 82/!! So I had to relinquish it. The one I got is from Peter Robinson, so is my coat. Mrs S.C. has bought two wonderful hats. One is a very high black bonnet with bunches of cock's feathers in the front. She looks like a million dollars in it, wizard. It is one of the 8 guinea hats I should think so is the other, navy blue halo with soft blue feathers. She has also bought a navy blue suit & a turquoise dress, so she is doing well. They are going to Germany, Switzerland & France this yr. lucky beggars.

You said that I didn't need to buy any summer frocks, I have no everyday ones, & only the green one Barbara passed on & the one I had made at Xmas, so I shall have to get 2.

Paddy, I have been discussing the allowance. Do you think £5 a month is too much? I know it won't be at college, & this term at school I have to buy

I am practising an Italian aria at the moment: o cessate di piegarmi .... that I am to sing on Wednesday evening. I am quaking at the thought.

Well goodbye darlings. Do take care of yourselves. Hebrews VI. God bless you.

Tons, tons of love
xxx xxxx xxx
ooo x x x x x Thea
C.S. I would love a sweater like this Mummy: buttoning all the way down the back, with ribbing at the round neck & cuffs, ends of sleeves, in turquoise, if it isn't too much trouble to make. 6b.) please Mummy a pretty hankie

turquoise
navy blue

Above left Letter from Thea to her parents, including sketches of Mrs Sydenham-Clarke's hats. 24 April 1947.

Above right Letter from Thea to her parents, including a drawing of a jumper she wanted her mother to make for her. 14 November 1948.

Keenly observant, especially about fashion, Thea wrote constantly about the clothes she saw people wearing, often providing little accompanying sketches. In a letter from April 1947, she remarked that: 'People are blossoming out into summer clothes. You see the most amazing sights in town. Black suits with heavy furs next to light silk and sandals.'[22] One day, she and her parents' friend Mrs Sydenham-Clarke were on the hunt for a hat: 'We went into about a dozen shops looking for a hat (*above*). In Oxford street, Piccadilly and Bond street ... I managed to get one for 31/ it is almost the same blue as my coat, a halo with bunches of ribbons on either side and floating strips of veiling hanging down on either side. Do you think it's too flashy? I tried on a dream of a hat, something like one of the hats that Princess Eliz. is wearing in South Africa, it really suited me ... S.C. has bought two wonderful hats. One is a very high black bonnet with bunches of cock's feathers in the front. She looks a million dollars in it, wizard.'[23]

Thea applied for Oxford and Cambridge but didn't get in; she was more successful however, with her application to Royal Holloway College where she started studying with great excitement in September 1947 aged 19, for a degree in French and Anglo-Saxon. In letters to her parents at this time, Thea expressed her concern about unrest in Damascus, but also talked of her studies and her friendships, especially with one of her closest of friends, Jacqueline Bullen (who would later become Venetia's godmother), of how mad they all were about clothes, and of the college dances to which the cadets from Sandhurst would be invited. Thea's mother sent her a 'pretty piece of crepe-georgette' for one of these dances, but as she didn't have time to 'drape it around the taffeta' she wore her 'cocktail frock' instead, drawing what she termed 'an odd assortment of frocks', using Jacqueline's lipstick for colour (*opposite*).[24]

February 1947 had seen the launch, by Christian Dior in Paris, of what came to be termed the New Look. Hugely successful, it caught on rapidly and by May 1948 Thea was asking her mother: 'Have you bought any new clothes and are they "new look". How are the Damascenes liking the new fuller skirts ... how sweet of you to buy me blue taffeta! It should be heavenly but I don't think it would do for that pattern. I shall try and get another pattern in London, something fuller ... not too little girlish (j'ai vingt ans petite maman!) with perhaps the suspicion of a bustle.'[25] In November (p.15) she wrote: 'I would love a sweater like this Mummy: buttoning all the way down the back with ribbing at the round neck and ends of sleeves, in turquoise! If it isn't too much trouble. And please mummy a pretty hankie.'[26]

Increasingly conscious of developing her style, Thea explained the colours she wanted to wear to her mother: 'Do you think you could buy me [from Beirut] some turquoise corduroy and make me a coat??? Rather the colour of the jumper you knitted me only more green. I thought I should work out a clothes colour scheme in navy blue & turquoise. I have a navy blue suit & I could get gloves & hat of turquoise. It would be heavenly. With turquoise one can also wear brown. I would love a brown taffeta semi-evening frock, is taffeta very expensive? I am enclosing a photo I cut out from Vogue of a pair of shoes to go with all this. I must have a high-heeled pair, all I have at the moment are the wide brown shoes you sent me which are too short in the toes ... I should like a three-inch heel, yes darling, don't topple over! THREE-INCH!'[27]

By the end of her second year at Royal Holloway, although her letters home do not hint at it, something was going wrong. She spent the summer of 1949 working in Foyles bookshop in London and did not return to her studies. Jacqueline recalls that they were all in shock and no one could tell them anything. Later, Thea explained simply that she was sent down for not working and 'summoned home in disgrace'.[28]

Opposite Letter from Thea to her parents, including drawings of the dresses worn at a dance at Royal Holloway College. 14 March 1949.

There was an odd assortment of frocks —
grey taffeta with a bustle + red bow + white broderie anglaise

[ermine

brocade

red moiré

the whole effect of this orange velvet (Jackie's hysterics)
was marred by a fall of white mosquito net all over! giving
a blurred effect.

pink gloves

black and white

white tulle heavenly!

yellow + mauve cheeks.

Well, goodbye darling. I hope you have enjoyed
this afternoon of a typical college dance.

All my love

Thea   xx xxxx
         x xx xx xx oo
         oo xx xxx oo

Beirut

Home was now to be Beirut, and so began a new phase of Thea's life: already glamorous, she now married, became a painter and developed a vibrant social life that revolved around the thriving artistic scene of Beirut in the 1950s and 1960s.

It was in the library of the British Embassy where she found work that Thea met Bob (Robert) Porter: 'a jolly bespectacled man not much taller than myself who had won a brilliant first at New College Oxford'[29] – he worked in the Development Division of the Embassy.[30] To her mother's horror on the day of the wedding she saw that Thea had rejected the cream brocade she had given her and was wearing something completely different (*below*): 'I had gone secretly to a dressmaker and had her run up a dress in white satin, embroidered with sequins and enlivened around the skirt with tufts of blue net … I designed this myself and looked and felt like a peacock.'[31]

Lebanon in this period was, like Syria, an independent country. Power groups with different religious affiliations (Sunni Muslim, Shi'i Muslim, Christian and Druze) all played a careful balancing act to maintain a fragile stability, which could easily dissolve as it did in 1958, sewing the seeds for the devastating Civil War of 1975–89.[32] However, Beirut during the 1950s and 1960s, was known as the Paris of the Middle East, or in Thea's words, 'a combination of Paris and Beverly Hills: the sex and glamour of the French capital allied to the hedonistic climate of California.'[33] Bob and Thea's social circle included Western and Lebanese politicians, journalists and artists, as well as the spy Kim Philby and his wife Eleanor,[34] while Bob's work also took them to Iraq and Jordan (where King Hussein awarded him a medal for his services to Jordan),[35] and once to Iran, where they met the Shah and

Opposite **Thea photographed in black evening dress. Lebanon, early 1950s.**

Right **Thea arriving at her wedding to Bob Porter. Beirut, 1952. Photograph by V. Derounian.**

Empress Soraya in the peacock throne-room. 'For the occasion I designed a dress, in the palest green and gold Indian silk gauze, short in front and longer in the back, which I considered the height of chic.'[36] Empress Soraya and the Shah's second wife Farah Pahlavi were later to become her customers (pp.53–4, 93).

Clothes played a huge part in Thea's life. In London she had to worry about how to pay for them, but now she prided herself on being the best-dressed embassy wife (although Bob would recall being staggered at her dressmaking bills).[37] In later years she recalled how 'Lebanese dressmakers bought couture toile and fabrics in Paris and sold line for line copies in Beirut.'[38] But as she was not able to afford these she describes how she had made 'a copy of a Lanvin dress with three layers of underpinnings, and a strapless Cardin dress in blue-grey taffeta with a cruelly boned and stiffened top, puffed out skirt and a hobble band around the knees. I looked like a meringue.'[39] She might visit the Beirut seamstresses with fabrics she had bought in the Beirut *suq* as often as three times a week: 'It was a sort of apprenticeship for what was to follow.'[40] One of her regular ports of call was also to a Russian woman called Madame Andrev, 'a fortune teller whose whispered predictions had a lot to do with my life-long addiction to soothsayers.'[41]

Socializing

Stylish socializing was *de rigeur*: there were parties at Bob and Thea's flat; there was coffee at the Horseshoe on Hamra; there were late evenings in bars and restaurants such as the Cave du Roy or L'Os; there were picnics in the mountains (*opposite*). As time went by, Bob travelled for work around the Middle East and Thea was constantly out. In an early version of her memoir she wrote: 'Two or three times a week I used to dine with the Prime Minister and a friend of his, a banker called Fadel Fadel, they both came from Tripoli in the north ... After dinner we would go from one cabaret to another ... it was fun to go from the grand Cave du Roy to really sleazy places. I loved that.'[42]

Nour Moura, whose family had worked for Thea's parents in Bloudan, now looked after Venetia, Thea's daughter (b.1955). She would come into Thea's room in the morning after these parties exclaiming: 'aren't you ashamed of yourself? I know what time you got back last night ... she would sit on my bed and harangue me about my increasingly wild friends and when one or other of them came to visit me she would say "the rubbish (*al-orta*) has arrived".'[43] The 'rubbish' consisted of a close-knit group of artists and writers, including the playwright Jalal Khoury (b.1934, who in his recollections of Thea described as her '*évanaissante*'),[44] Aimée Khoury (editor of the literary journal *Le Reveil*), as well as artists Paul Guiragossian (1925–93) and Aref Rayyes (1928–2005), who at a party at their flat one night 'did a leap worthy of Nureyev and landed precariously on my mantelpiece'.[45]

Above Thea at the Cave du Roy. The photograph was made into a souvenir matchbox. Beirut, early 1960s.

Right Thea and husband Bob Porter at a diplomatic function. Beirut, early 1960s.

Below Venetia and her Syrian nanny Nour Moura at the beach. Beirut, about 1958.

Right Thea and friends at a nightclub. Beirut, early 1960s.

Below right A picnic in the mountains of Lebanon (includes Khaldun al-Hosri, Bob Porter, Aline Flash and Venetia Porter). Photograph by Thea's brother Patrick Seale. On the reverse Thea wrote 'Je n'étais pas si gaie que ça' ('I was not as light-hearted as I looked').

Art

Thea was close to these and other artists, such as the Syrian painter Fateh Moudarres (1922–99) and Khalil Zgheib (1911–75, *below*). Zgheib was a remarkable painter, a barber by trade, who was entirely self-taught.[46] He painted scenes of village life and landscapes on hardboard, and his work so inspired Thea that in 1971 she commissioned Sandra Munro to design a textile based on one of his paintings that she owned (*opposite*).

This period of her life was integral to her later work as a designer; it was a time when she 'struggled to understand how colours and forms could be balanced and welded together'.[47] Thea's interactions with her artist friends helped her to define her own colour palette, and in 1957, she began studying under Georges Cyr (1881–1964), who had lived in Lebanon since 1934 and was credited with the revival of 'Lebanese' art, and then Madame Aubry Beaulieu (1917–2006), wife of Paul André Beaulieu (the Canadian Ambassador to Lebanon), who was an accomplished artist in her own right.[48]

Thea had four exhibitions altogether between 1959 and 1963, but it was the last two, in 1961 and 1963 at the Alecco Saab gallery,[49] from which there are the most detailed records and where it is clear that her style was becoming distinctive and well defined. Her paintings were abstract and full of colour; she worked on paper and on canvas, often using collage, mirror and gold leaf. The writer Michel Fani described her work as having echoes of Pop Art mixed with local popular culture.[50] In an interview in *al-Usbu' al-Arabi* regarding Thea's 1961 show, the journalist asks her about that element of popular culture which Fani refers to – the preponderance of 'the eye' in her paintings – to which Thea replied: 'I believe in the eye, I fear the eye of envy

Left Playwright Jalal Khoury (right), artist Khalil Zgheib (centre), and Mexican Ambassador Rodolpho Usigli. Beirut, early 1960s.

Right Chiffon top and headdress printed with a design, by Sandra Munro, based on a landscape painting by the Lebanese artist Khalil Zgheib (*below*). British *Vogue*, April 1975. Photograph by Barry Lategan.

Below Khalil Zgheib, *Landscape by a River*. Oil on hardboard, probably early 1960s. Venetia Porter collection.

Right Georges Cyr and Simone Aubry Beaulieu, Thea's two art teachers, at the opening of her exhibition at the Alecco Saab gallery in Beirut, 1961.

Below Thea in front of one of her paintings, 1963.

Right Thea at the opening of her exhibition at the Alecco Saab gallery in 1963, with Sir Moore Crosthwaite (left), British Ambassador

... don't forget that I was born in the Middle East.'[51] This belief in the power of the evil eye would remain with Thea throughout her life: the invitation to her 1968 show was the protective 'Hand of Fatima' (see p.71) in the palm of which was the 'unblinking eye', 'reflecting' she wrote 'my enduring if feeble-minded interest in clairvoyants, astrologers and soothsayers.'[52]

Leaving for London

Thea's 1963 exhibition was also well received,[53] but by now she was feeling restless: her marriage was not working and she'd had at least one affair. She wrote later that 'her innocent childhood of Syria was being eroded by the corrupting influence of Beirut.'[54] 'I left Beirut in May 1964, a Beirut of ceaseless parties, beautiful days on beaches long picnics in the mountains every Sunday; mornings drinking coffee at the Horseshoe ... It was too much pleasure I felt I had to work ... The night before I left some of my painter and gallery friends had a dinner for me at L'Os. They had always teased me about being a gifted amateur painter and embassy wife.' On a scrap of napkin they awarded Thea the Nobel Prize for friendship and with that, she left for London.

Below Thea Porter,
Untitled. Gouache and
gold leaf on paper, 1962.
Abstract painting showing
a glass bead against the
'evil eye' at lower right.
Venetia Porter collection.

Opposite Thea Porter,
Untitled. Oil on canvas,
early 1960s. Venetia Porter
collection.

27   Damascus & Beirut

'I really think that Syria is a most beautiful country. Every time I close my eyes it's there. It haunts me.'

Damascus and Beirut:
Design inspiration and the Middle East
Laura McLaws Helms

Thea Porter's nostalgia for the Middle East remained with her throughout her life.[1] Using textile designs, and then couture, she was able to keep alive this chimerical world. Thea's creative vision and unique signature style proved her to be a designer whose inspirations were broad and constantly evolving, yet they were also based on thorough research.[2]

Though she was part of a renaissance in British fashion design spearheaded by a group of designers, including Zandra Rhodes and Bill Gibb, who also found inspiration in other cultures and history, Porter's designs were singular and distinctive. Her revisions of Middle Eastern dress blended fashion with tradition, and were produced to a high quality with luxury and antique fabrics, which separated her designs (*opposite*) from trendy mass-market examples. Porter's unique use of actual world textiles developed from her fascination with, in particular, Islamic textiles such as the *suzani* embroideries and *ikat*s of Central Asia, Ottoman velvets and the embroidered textiles and brocades of Damascus that she saw in her childhood. While it was uncommon for Western designers to use such fabrics, precedents can be found as early as the 1920s in the work of the House of Reville.[3]

As a designer, Porter was remarkably discerning when it came to the work of her peers. She showed little interest in all but a select few, but she loved, and was particularly inspired by, the work of two earlier designers, Paul Poiret (1879–1944) and Mariano Fortuny (1871–1949), whose early twentieth-century designs dramatically changed women's dress (*overleaf*). Fortuny was not a conventional fashion designer, as he worked outside the fashion system of seasonal collections, but the Middle Eastern textiles and costumes his artist father collected as studio props heavily inspired his designs (now housed in the Fortuny Museum in Venice).[4] In her memoir, Thea wrote: 'Fortuny was one of the major influences on modern fashion, only rivalled by his great contemporary, Paul Poiret. [They] freed women from corsets long before Chanel … and Poiret introduced the *soutien gorge*, the bra.'[5]

Thea felt a particular affinity for Poiret, 'he re-created the Arabian Nights in Paris … and dressed Mata Hari for the stage. His salon was strewn with

floor cushions, his assistants were dressed in furs … like me, he adored Turkish trousers, turbans, tassels and kimono blouses.'[6] Drawing on Fortuny's work (he invented a silk pleating process to make his 'Delphos' gowns, as well as a technique for stencil-printing the finest silk velvets for his capes and mantels),[7] Porter began to include pleated silk chiffon capes in her collection in 1972 – these theatrical floor-length pieces were printed with peacocks (see p.78–9) or colour blocked.[8] Such Fortuny-esque pleating was also seen in the work of Porter's American contemporary, Mary McFadden (b.1938), who began experimenting in the mid-1970s with techniques to achieve pleats that held their creases. McFadden developed a synthetic pleated satin that she trademarked, and which became her signature design throughout her career; Porter's pleating however, appeared only

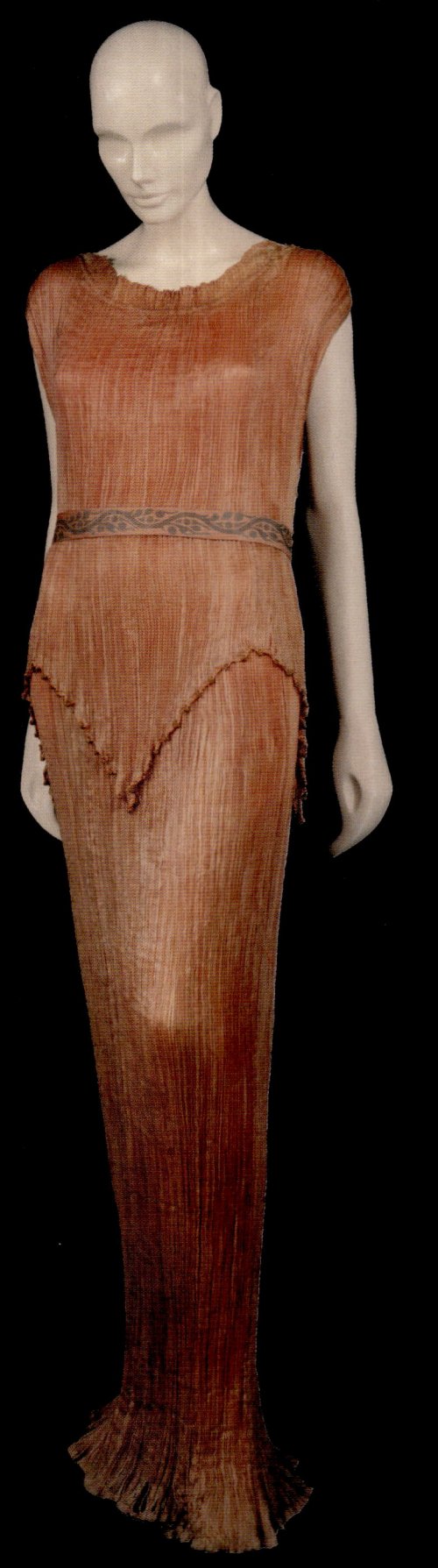

Left Known for designing clothes that allowed women to abandon the corset, Mariano Fortuny developed a technique for pleating silk that maintained its shape. His 'Delphos' gown harked back to the classical Greek *chiton*; glass beads on the hem meant that the elastic pleating clung to the body and draped gracefully. Porter greatly admired Fortuny, describing him as 'one of the major influences on modern fashion.'
V&A: T.193&A–1974

intermittently in her collections. In her Autumn/Winter 1978–9 collection, pleated silk dresses and scarves were showcased alongside languid velvet sheaths, replicating Fortuny textiles and silhouettes, while in 1979 it reappeared in the form of spangled chiffon mini-dresses and long pleated satin tassels hanging from belts. An August 1980 letter from Marylou Luther, then-fashion editor at the *Los Angeles Times*, congratulates Porter for 'scooping' Yves Saint Laurent on the use of 'Fortuny pleats',[9] as the French designer would include them in his collection that year.

Contemporaries

Of all the designers working contemporaneously with Thea, she was most fond of the British menswear tailor Tommy Nutter (1943–92, see p.99), yet the work of Yves Saint Laurent (1936–2008) shared the greatest similarity of theme and voice with her own.[10] Both designers were born and brought up in Arab countries, and both incorporated memories of their original homes into their designs. While Saint Laurent considered himself French, Algeria was his homeland and when conscripted to fight on the French side in the war with Algeria in 1960, he was so conflicted that he had a nervous breakdown, fuelled in part by the psychological impossibility of fighting against the land and people from which his creative mind-set had been forged. Saint Laurent and Porter had no recorded personal interactions, but dressed many of the same women. Saint Laurent's designs stayed within the bounds of traditional Western fashion until his 'African' collection of 1967, but he did not truly push the bounds of fashion fantasy until his 'Ballet Russes' *haute couture* collection for Autumn/Winter 1976–7. Described by the *New York Times* as the 'apogee of "rich hippie" bohemian style'[11] (a name actually coined by Marylou Luther to describe Porter's work), this collection was awash with exotic gipsy influences, harking back to much of the work Porter had been producing in London over the previous decade. Though it is unknown whether Saint Laurent was inspired by Porter's work directly, it is highly likely that he was aware of her designs.

Thea and Saint Laurent both advocated a look steeped in nostalgia, whether for nineteenth-century Orientalism or the 1940s. Many of Porter's contemporaries in London also referenced historical designs in their work, with fashion in the late 1960s and early 1970s taking on a romantic and fantastical edge.[12] Gina Fratini (b.1931), a London-based designer, brought up in Japan, revisioned Kate Greenaway-esque shepherdesses of the late nineteenth century, which in turn were dressed in late eighteenth-century garb; while the Scotsman Bill Gibb (1943–88) plundered medieval and Renaissance modes – a style Porter referenced freely in 1970 with a collection of tapestry-printed velvets and slash sleeved gowns (p.32). Though Thea lived and designed apart from the rest of the London fashion scene, she shared with Gibb a love of textiles and ornamentation that resulted in

*Emb cheesecloth
cream voile sleeves,
trimmed red roses*

a certain affinity of taste: both also worked with the textile designer Janet Taylor (b.1936) who remembers their similarly exacting natures as well as the general and chaotic disorganization of their businesses.[13]

Just as Thea saw textiles as the starting point for her work, so too did her contemporary Zandra Rhodes (b.1940). A trained textile designer, Rhodes launched her own high-end fashion line in 1969, creating romantic, voluminous designs that provided the ideal canvases for her unique prints. Likewise, Ossie Clark (1942–96) used specially designed textiles to transmute his masterfully tailored designs into romantic confections. Clark's use of cut and print marked him as the star of the London fashion scene in the late 1960s and early 1970s. Rhodes, Clark and Porter shared a love of fabric, but also an engagement with other cultures and an inherent interest in using dress as a form of costume: in other words, fashion as a conduit to fantasy.

Barbara Hulanicki's career at the helm of the London label Biba in the 1960s and 1970s was influenced by the same connections with the Middle East as Thea and Saint Laurent: born in Warsaw, Hulanicki (b.1936) was brought up in Palestine before moving to England when she was 12. Whereas Hulanicki's Biba style was more a fusion of pop culture that acknowledged an Oriental fantasy, her success was at least as dependent on the idea of the East as it was to actual and authentic forms and objects. Both Porter and Hulanicki appealed to the burgeoning tastes for exoticism, but the Biba look

Above left **Romantic silhouettes, with full Victorian skirts and puffed sleeves, appeared throughout Porter's career. This example is sketched in white cheesecloth with red rose trim.**

Above right **Porter's flair for historicism is particularly evident in the two dresses on the left (the dress on the right is by Bellville Sassoon). Modelled by the Percy sisters (Lady Caroline, Lady Julia and Lady Victoria). British *Vogue*, October 1970. Photograph by Barry Lategan.**

hit the high streets with Westernized imagery of dreamy romantic heroines more likely to appear in the trendy hippy circles of Chelsea, whereas Porter sold more authentic fashion and interior décor. Biba opened several outlets in Kensington in the mid-to-late 1960s (described as 'the most exotic shop in London' by *Vanity Fair*), where Hulanicki cultivated her interest in mysterious and dramatic interiors,[14] using wallpapers and interiors that were a modern and decadent reworking of Art Nouveau style mixed with Middle Eastern flavour. Both Porter and Hulanicki were interested in the idea of the 'total look', where fashion and lifestyle were seen as constant and continuous reflections of each other, to be sold and used as one (*below*).

The main difference between Biba and designers such as Porter, Rhodes and Gibb was the price tag. Far beyond the salary of a 'normal' shopper, Porter's designs were the exclusive purview of the wealthy. This meant that

Right Biba's department store, Big Biba, opened in 1973 and included the exotic 'Casbah Room', which sold North African and Middle Eastern goods. Photographed in Barbara Hulanicki's own home, this poster advertised the launch of the shop. Poster by Steve Thomas.
V&A: AAD/1996/6/57/1

her clientele was also often in their thirties or older. While Porter did in fact have young clients, these women were usually celebrities or socialites. Usually quite forgiving in cut, Porter's clothes felt luxurious as well as comfortable: in a market that had shifted to focus predominantly on youth, these were all appealing traits to a discerning woman who wanted to look fabulous, attractive and demonstrate her good taste.

Indeed, Porter's pieces were priced to be affordable only by those with disposable income. This exclusivity was enhanced by the fact that they were primarily made to order and only available from a small shop off the beaten track. Biba, conversely, piled clothes high to sell quickly and cheaply. Porter's clothes were aspirational to her clientele, intended to flatter with cut and seductive fabrics, which emphasized the sophisticated taste of the wearer. More than anything it was the transformative power of her designs that was so appealing: the Sri Lankan-born socialite Helga De Silva Blow Perera remembers how 'Thea Porter's clothes pulsate with exotic energy. "Wearing her" apart from energizing [me], immediately transported me back from the grey and coldness of the west to the warm tropical island where I come from.'[15] It was this unique energy – a confluence of exotic colours, shapes and textiles – that gave Thea's designs the power to seduce and invigorate her clients.

With most of her garments being custom-made, and therefore almost singular works of art, Porter's approach to fashion design seems to embody Poiret's maxim that, 'nothing seems to me better nor more beautiful than to express in colours, as if they were primal cries, all the emotion that is caused in one by the contemplation of nature' in all its aspects.[16] Discussing her own creative process, Porter wrote:

Every designer, every artist, has to believe that he or she has come up with something new, but the truth is that we are all the product of outside influences, many of them absorbed unconsciously. There is a sense in which nothing is new, except in the rearrangement of images inherited from the past, and passed through the sieve of one's own feelings and sensibility.[17]

Right Model wearing white embroidered *abaya*, pictured in a French chateau. *L'Officiel*, no. 628, December 1976. Photograph by Patrick Bertrand.

The seven 'Signature' garments

In her memoir Porter describes several of the most important garments or styles she designed.[18] The following seven garments illustrate not only her best-selling styles, but also the styles that Porter herself felt the greatest affinity for: the *abaya*, the Gipsy dress, the Faye dress, a brocade dress with sheer side panels, a wrap-over dress, the Chazara jacket and a *sirwal*-like skirt. While Porter was known for her exotic and Middle Eastern-inspired fashion, not all of these pieces express those connections. Although her designs did take on a more classically European form during the 1970s (in keeping with a general shift in fashion trends away from the hippie styles of the late 1960s towards a more 'retro' style that looked to the 1930s and 1940s for inspiration), Porter was still producing reworkings of her signature *abayas* for each collection.[19]

Abayas and kaftans

Probably the best known of all of Porter's designs is based upon the *abaya* (*opposite*) often described as a *kaftan* or *djellaba* in museum collections or at auctions of vintage clothes. Technically, an *abaya* is a voluminous, all-covering robe, generally black, worn by women primarily in the Arabian Peninsula,[20] which is made either from a large square of fabric with slits for the head and hands, or else more tailored, in the style of a loose dress. *Abayas* can have a divided or closed front, and are almost always black and undecorated; *kaftan* is a Persian word that describes a full-length robe with long sleeves that buttons down the front; *djellaba* most commonly describes a hooded loose outer robe worn in North Africa.[21]

The influx of various Middle Eastern and North African traditional garments into Western Europe in the 1960s, brought back from the hippie trail, resulted in any vaguely Arabic-looking robe being referred to as a 'kaftan'. The question of what to call 'ethnic' garments was even broached in the British press in 1968:[22] remarking on the success of 'the trendy *kaftan*, the brash *burnous*, the Mao collar and the jolly *jodpuri*,' Christopher Ward concluded that: 'Unfortunately, no one is able to agree about what any of these items of Eastern promise exactly are.'[23]

The first garments that Porter ever made were *kaftan*s: an article from January 1967 shows a man modelling one of the antique *kaftan*s sold in her shop, which she began to replicate.[24] These *kaftan*s were floor-length with long sleeves, a standing collar and a slim body. The reworking of North African and Middle Eastern traditional dress has a long history in Western fashion: the opening up of trade in the seventeenth and eighteenth centuries brought sumptuous goods from the East, which influenced Western dress in form and pattern, yet this fascination can be traced back even further to Marco Polo's travels in the late thirteenth century.[25] The simple, straight cut of the *kaftan* was seen by some early twentieth century *haute couturiers* –

Above **Moyra Swan in a sheer *abaya* over a tight-fitting black bodysuit. Topkapı Palace, Istanbul. British *Vogue*, November 1971. Photograph by Barry Lategan.**

the foremost being the French designer Paul Poiret – as a rejection of the highly shaped Western fashions of the period, and they would later inspire the mid-1960s designs of Balenciaga (1895–1972) and Yves Saint Laurent.[26]

Porter's attraction to the *abaya* lay in its enveloping fabric: 'I've always felt very envious of Arab women because they can hide behind their clothes. It is a very protected and secure way to feel.'[27] Contemporary Middle Eastern dress was largely unknown in the West until the oil crisis of 1973 when press coverage of oil-producing countries brought an increased awareness of the cultures of the region. Up until this point, examples of Middle Eastern dress in American and Western European popular culture were derived mainly from Hollywood's fascination with the 'Orient' in the 1920s, which was based on stylized and fantastical stereotypes. This could be seen in films such as Rudolph Valentino's *The Sheik* (1921), and later in the multi-cultural pillaging of the San Francisco hippies – neither era being interested in

Opposite Elizabeth Taylor bought *abayas* from several designers, but during the mid-1970s most came from Thea Porter. Thirteen of the pieces (including the first two in the arrangement here) were auctioned by Christie's in 2011.

Right Sketched on to an envelope that held the pattern pieces, this illustration shows an *abaya* with patchwork corners and belted waist. V&A: AAD/1995/4/1

Far right A devoré velvet open-fronted version of the *abaya*, 1977. Illustration by Duthy. V&A: AAD/1995/4/34

authenticity, but instead solely concerned with the look of the garments. In her voluminous *abayas* and *thawb*s,[28] Porter was alluding to the importance of modesty in Islamic culture, and the harshness of the climate: 'the garments from the hot interior of Arabia are far more loosely cut and have large, spacious sleeves.'[29]

It is unclear when Porter first made her version of the *abaya*, but it was likely within her first two years of designing, and certainly by November 1971, when the first *abaya* appeared in the pages of British *Vogue*. The editorial (shot by Barry Lategan in Turkey) exploited the trend for ethnic-inspired dress, photographing models as whirling dervishes amid 'troglodyte dwellings' and tiled wall palaces.[30] Silhouetted against the Istanbul skyline, the sheer black georgette *abaya* is enlivened by the breeze, emphasizing both the lightness of the fabric and the slender frame of the leotard-clad model beneath (p.37).

At least 25 versions of Porter's *abaya* dress were made, including 'some with hoods, some without. Some had knotted sleeves, as in an eighteenth-century portrait by Moroni, others were of Chinese inspiration',[31] and they generated remarkable commercial success: they were popular for their ability to hide the body beneath the billowing folds, with transparent fabrics hinting subtly at the female form. Traditionally made in the Middle East in lightweight black wool with no decoration, the *abaya* was transformed in Porter's hands, which made it ideal for her Middle Eastern clients.[32] Her *abayas* also had fans among Western women – notably Elizabeth Taylor (see *opposite*). The voluminous and highly embellished type of *abaya* also appeared in the collections of Porter's contemporaries, including

Zandra Rhodes, who enjoyed great success in Hollywood with it. The large swathes of fabric on the *abaya* provided Rhodes with an open canvas for exhibiting her textile designs, in much the same way that Porter could use them to show off fine antique textiles.[33]

Concurrently with the *abaya*, Porter was constantly evolving the *kaftan* as well as the *djellaba*. One design, described by British *Vogue* as a 'tobacco chiffon caftan with smoked gold leaves, hooded, boot-buttoned, Arabic sleeves weighed with tassels', combines the hood of the *djellaba* with the slimmer cut of the *kaftan*.[34] Similar in cut to some of the heavily brocaded Ottoman *kaftans* in the collection of Topkapı Palace in Istanbul, Turkey,[35] this particular Porter design (*above*) is made of silk, transparent and gossamer thin, leaving no illusions about the body beneath. A gold rope belt encircles the waist tightly. The whole effect is one of Orientalist splendour, recalling the work of nineteenth-century painters such as Eugène Delacroix

Above Anne Schaufuss in a brown and gold button-front hooded *djellaba* with hanging, tassled sleeves. The organza and velvet dress on the right is also by Thea Porter. British *Vogue*, December 1970. Photograph by Clive Arrowsmith.

(1798–1863) and Théodore Géricault (1791–1824).[36] Variations on the slimmer *kaftan* were modelled by Swedish starlet Britt Ekland in a British *Vogue* editorial from February 1969; she was photographed in a full-length coat version, in white jute with gold braid, and an open, belted robe with a high slit at the sides, scalloped edges and floor-length sleeves.[37]

Described as 'medieval', the dangling sleeves of these garments echo the late fourteenth- and early fifteenth-century *houppelande* (a robe usually featuring long, trailing sleeves)[38] as well as the traditional dresses from villages around Damascus[39] and nineteenth-century Turkish overdresses.[40] Perhaps related, and in a similar vein, Porter's art teacher in Beirut, Georges Cyr, illustrated a volume of Lebanese and Syrian traditional costume: among the leaves detailing men and women's dress are several *kaftan*s with similar dangling sleeves and embellished plackets.

Right **Georges Cyr, 'Bedouin Woman of the Orontes Plain' in** *Liban, Costumes et Paysages,* **1940s. Porter incorporated many features of Middle Eastern traditional dress, including the hanging sleeves and yoked dress seen in her teacher Cyr's drawing.**

Opposite and right This *abaya* synthesizes an oversized print (possibly by Michael Szell) based on Persian tile designs with Damascus brocade patchwork corners. Mid-1970s. Lauren Lepire collection. Photograph by Amanda Charchian.

The Gipsy dress

This dress was produced in three main variations: the keyhole Gipsy (*below*), the scoop-necked Gipsy and the crossover Gipsy. First designed in 1968, according to Porter, the Gipsy was 'generally made out of a combination of three different fabrics, which gave it an enduring variety. If the skirt was in plain cotton, the bodice was usually in brocade … We made the dress in every conceivable fabric, from embroidered chiffon, to Liberty cottons to velvet.'[41] The basic silhouette draws on Eastern European and Mediterranean folk costume, which in the eighteenth and nineteenth centuries was composed of a billowing-sleeved chemise, a full skirt and an apron.[42] The cut and decoration of these garments differed from region to region, but every piece in the ensemble was frequently embroidered; a cloak or jacket would traditionally have been worn for protection against the elements, and small vests or fitted bodices evolved over time, which were worn over the chemise.[43] The silhouette of a slimmer torso combined with full skirt (composed of 4.5 metres of fabric) and sleeves became the basis for Porter's Gipsy dress.[44]

Left **The Gipsy dress, first designed in 1968, came in many variations. This sketch of the keyhole Gipsy was made by one of Thea's assistants to show clients. V&A: AAD/1995/4/13**

Right Gipsy dress made for Venetia Porter's twenty-first birthday. It includes a chainmail bodice, lace sleeves, a printed chiffon skirt and velvet ribbon trim. Venetia Porter collection.

Above Actress Sharon Tate
arriving at a party with
Peter Sellers. She wears
a Gipsy dress with moiré
bodice and polka-dot
chiffon skirt and sleeves.
Tate had placed a large
order with Porter the
previous month. London,
1 July 1969.

The Gipsy inspiration probably comes from the ways in which Gipsy women layered different patterns and textiles when dressing, as well as their penchant for full floral skirts. Turkic peoples wore variations on a fitted over-bodice or vest, and it is likely that it was one of these that Porter adapted for the cut of her Gipsy dress, with the vest becoming an integrated part of the bodice, ending directly below the breasts to create an empire line. The cut is such that the bust is held in securely, yet pushed up, removing the necessity of wearing a bra. Perhaps because of its figure-enhancing lift, Porter's Gipsy dresses were a success with starlets who enjoyed its enticing effect (*opposite*). The uneven hem of the Gipsy dress evolved as a form of collaboration between Thea and one of her first seamstresses, Meg Lake, who was self-taught and didn't realise that a circle of fabric cut on the bias would fall irregularly and need to be trimmed. Porter loved that effect and the mistake became a design signature.[45] The crossover Gipsy featured trim that circled the neckline to cross at the centre-front and cup the bust; the same bodice was used on a number of other dresses, usually with bands that defined the wearer's chest and a tiered skirt.

Porter referenced the Russian avant-garde artist Natalia Goncharova in her description of the Gipsy dress,[46] but she was also greatly influenced by Léon Bakst, the artistic director of the Ballets Russes, who was responsible for some of their most fantastical costumes. For Porter, the turn of the nineteenth century and the early twentieth century were the most interesting and inspiring periods in history:

Rather than looking at clothes of past decades for inspiration, I prefer to look at paintings of the [Art Deco] period. In a Van Dongen portrait of a French beauty at Deauville or Paris, you can almost stroke the velvet or the satin and inhale the rich mingling of scent and Russian cigarettes, a burst of exoticism which in turn owed a great deal to Léon Bakst, the revolutionary Russian theatrical designer who took Paris by storm early this century with his designs for Diaghilev's Russian ballet.[47]

Bakst's costumes for *Schéhérazade* (1910, *above*) were unquestionably a great influence on Porter's Gipsy dress: the high, tight bodices with floating, transparent skirts in an assortment of jewel tones and patterns, trimmed with ribbons and gold, became integral to her designs. Porter usually had these dresses made up from three different fabrics, with the bodice often crafted in an antique brocaded silk. An evening Gipsy dress might have a brocaded silk bodice with a shot silk skirt and sleeves, and velvet ribbon trim. The brocaded bodice might be paired with thin printed muslin, one colour for the sleeves and skirt with another for the hem. For her ill-fated ready-to-wear line, Porter designed a day version of printed cotton voile with gold braid trim (see p.91).

The Faye dress

In contrast to the Gipsy, the Faye dress was high-necked with flowing sleeves, a full skirt and a tight bodice. Named for her client, the American actress Faye Dunaway, it was usually made of sheer georgette in a rainbow of colours with a panel of antique brocade covering the chest, above a tight, wide belt of the same fabric. The Faye was continually remade in several variations from 1968 onwards, and was a notable success. Porter reminisced later that: 'One night at Elaine's in New York I saw Betty Bacall and Jane Fonda both wearing the Faye dress, luckily in different colours.'[48] Constructed from white lace, the Faye dress made for an ideal wedding gown; Thea described the dress as 'nun-like and all-enveloping', yet the transparency of the fabric revealed more than the cut supposed – balancing the design cleverly between modesty and romanticism.[49]

Below left Susanne Elliott at her wedding in a lace Faye dress with long scalloped veil. Lincoln, 21 March 1970.

Below right Lace Faye dress with devoré velvet bodice and two bands of velvet trim at the hem; silk organza veil also trimmed in velvet. Worn by Susanne Elliott at her wedding. V&A: T.46:1 to 3–2005

Right **A Faye dress from 1970, featuring a high neck, brocade bodice and printed chiffon skirt. V&A: T.900–2000**

Brocade panel dress

The play between masking and revelation also appeared in the next dress in Porter's list of key garments: 'a long slim dress with brocade panels front and back, with see-through sides, the brocade was edged with thin braid or ribbon.'[50] Described by *Women's Wear Daily* as a 'caftan', this dress was first produced in 1971 and was ordered in multiple colourways by socialites including Veronique Peck and Betsy Whitney.[51] Like Salome's veils these dresses shrouded the form yet allowed for tantalizing glimpses of the figure beneath (*above*).

Right Thea Porter, sketch of wrap-over dress. Combining the lean lines of the 1940s with the wrapped effect and sleeves of the kimono, this dress was elegant and easy to wear. V&A: AAD/1995/4/13

Crossover dress with sleeves to the floor it made women look as slim as the sleeve

Wrap-over dress

Possibly the most glamorous of all of Porter's key garments, the wrap-over dress with sleeves to the floor was designed to make women look as slim as the sleeve itself (their dripping length creates the optical illusion of a body equally as long and lean). These dresses, which varied in style, were easy to wear and feather light, yet provided an elegance that far surpassed their slender form (*opposite*). The designer remembered: 'we made it in pierrot green and in pink, in black and in gold. Queen Farah [Pahlavi], who saw the dress in Geneva, sent an emissary to me in London to ask if I could make her one.'[52] The American model Jan de Villeneuve, who often worked for Porter in the mid-1970s, remarked of the gown's cascading sleeves: 'It's certainly not practical but it's incredibly beautiful.'[53] The spangled fabric that Porter favoured for these gowns (and other similar styles in the mid-1970s) was impossible to dry-clean or wash without losing much of the glued-on glitter, and so these dresses represented a rareness and ephemerality even beyond the norm for couture.

Chazara jacket

My favourite clothes are jackets to wear with trousers or a skirt: I prefer separates as you can contrive to wear them all day and all evening too. Shirley [sic] Fonda had about forty, brocade and velvet blazers, narrow jackets with big puffed sleeves cut on an Arab pattern; jackets in striped silk velvet, in sequins; embroidered at the string neck with beaded roses, we made hundreds. I love men's jackets with patch pockets, remade in thin gold and black silk velvet. Or small tops to the waist in lace, edged in silver braid that is finished with hand crochet in gold.[54]

The hip-length, long-line tunic jacket with a Nehru collar, beloved by women such as American socialite Shirlee Fonda, was called the 'Chazara' after a type of butterfly, and was produced in a multitude of different fabrics: lace, velvet and brocaded silk (*opposite*). The jackets featured a banded effect that was created using ribbons and antique braids sewn down the front.[55] On the back, the expertly cut pattern pieces were edged with silk piping to produce geometric shapes and a long and lean silhouette. Taking inspiration from eighteenth-century military coats (*opposite*), the Chazara jacket replicates the linear application of trim seen in costumes designed by Bakst for *The Sleeping Princess* ballet in 1921. The Chazara jacket was introduced to the collection in 1975, refining the design of one of Porter's earlier trouser suits (c.1968), which included a hip-length, tunic-style jacket with a standing collar and braid trim (p.56). Faye Dunaway 'would pop in unannounced to buy a clutch of pantsuits in five or six different colours, braided like a band uniform.'[56]

Opposite, clockwise from top left **Madras jacket made for photographer Justin de Villeneuve following his marriage to one of Porter's favourite models, Jan Ward, in 1975. Porter continued to make clothes for men into the 1970s. Jan de Villeneuve collection.**

Chazara **jacket sketch by Thea Porter. An immediate hit, the jacket combined ease of wear with endless variety through different combinations of fabrics and trims.**

Chazara **jacket worn with black spangled turban and red taffeta skirt.** *Country Life*, **6 March 1975. Photograph by Alec Murray.**

Costume for a Huntsman from *The Sleeping Princess* **by Marius Petipa, after Léon Bakst. Metallic trim tracing the lines of the body and opulent fabrics offer the same luxurious military styling as Porter's** *Chazara* **jacket. Made for the Ballets Russes, 1921. V&A: S.119–1981**

'I believe very strongly in clothes being casual: I think they should be unpadded, and easy to wear.'

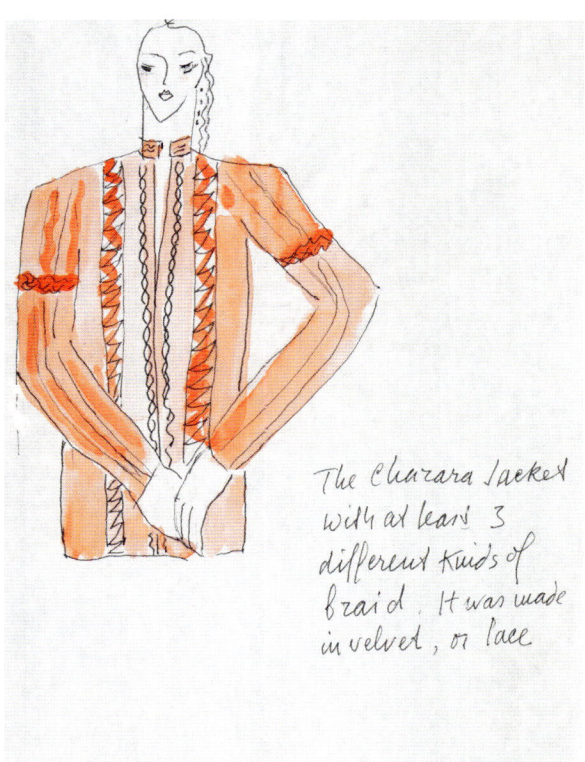

The charara Jacket
with at least 3
different Kinds of
braid. It was made
in velvet, or lace

Left Velvet waistcoat with Syrian-style embroidery and knickerbockers, 1968. It would have been worn with a sheer silk blouse. Cherie Federau collection.

Opposite Chazara jacket in silver lace with antique silver braid. Laura McLaws Helms collection. Photograph by Amanda Charchian.

Sirwal skirt

The final key Porter piece was her *sirwal* skirt (*below*). Drawing on the traditional *sirwal* (baggy pyjama-like trousers) worn in Lebanon and the Arabian Peninsula,[57] Porter reinterpreted them into a tightly waisted skirt with voluminous draped folds that fell either to the knee or the ankle. With a silhouette reminiscent of harem odalisques in Orientalist paintings,[58] this skirt bridged the gap between fantasy and modernity: it was made from jersey, and so was easy to both wear and pack, and therefore particularly appealing to Porter's jet-set clientele. This draped silhouette reappeared throughout her collections over the years, in a variety of textiles. Adaptations of the exotic *sirwal* have been shown in collections of European-based designers for over a century, from Poiret (who introduced full 'jupe-culottes' in 1911 to be worn under a long tunic) to the British Iranian designer Shirin Guild (b.1946; who has been producing 'Tribal' loose trousers since the mid-1980s).[59]

Although Porter did not include outerwear in the list of her most important designs, the textiles she selected for their construction, and compelling cuts she employed when piecing them together, deserve a mention. A series of coats made from heavy crewel-embroidered textiles were presented in the Autumn/Winter 1970 collection. Described by British

Below left Sketch of Thea Porter's *sirwal* skirt (spelt here as '*sarwal*'). Based on Middle Eastern style trousers, it was introduced in the mid-1970s and appeared in collections well into the 1980s. V&A: AAD/1995/4/10

Below right In her Autumn/Winter 1982 collection, Thea Porter contrasted the *sirwal* skirt in silk with a brocade jacket and matching turban. Photograph by Van Pariser.

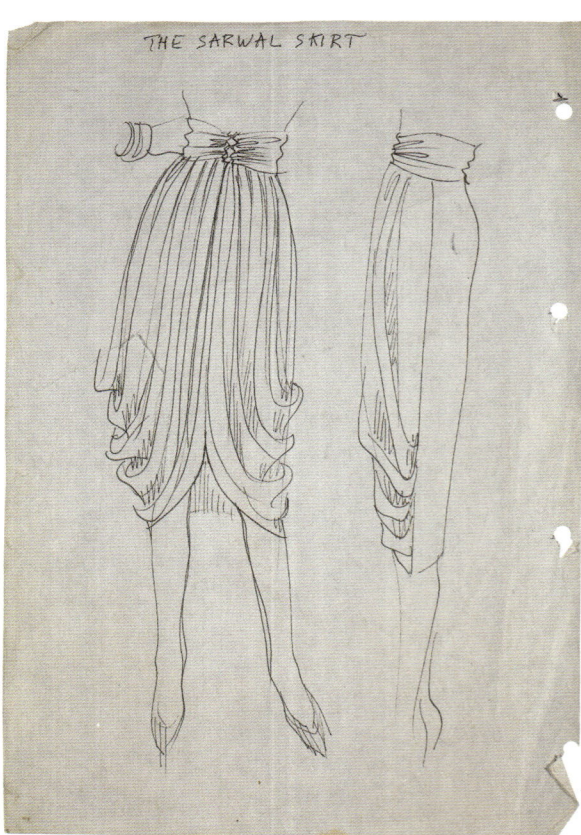

THE SARWAL SKIRT

Vogue as 'a mosaic of carpet embroidery,'[60] the textiles were probably hook-embroidered rugs or bedcovers in their original form. Porter's favourites included the brightly woven rugs of southern Iraq, with traditional apricot-coloured wool embroidered in chain stitch in woollen yarns of orange, red, green and white.[61] She originally imported them to make them into shoulder bags and cushion covers, and then fashioned them into coats.[62] The applied decoration was laid out in an ordered pattern, as with the stripes of motifs seen on a coat featured in British *Vogue*. Porter was so fond of this design that she then asked Sandra Munro to turn it into a textile that was subsequently used to make a wide array of garments from trouser suits to Gipsy dresses (*above*).

Like much of her work, these key pieces feature multi-cultural influences, sometimes authentic in style and silhouette, while at other times filtered through, and combined with, a Western European fashion aesthetic. Thea's childhood and young adult life in Damascus and Beirut impacted not just on the silhouettes and textiles she used, but also informed the way she interacted with other cultures. Choosing not to see each culture as singular and separate, she found inspiration and excitement in the way they blended and merged. Her keen eye, her design sense and her style as it developed during her early London years, were enhanced by that complex heritage. By translating her earlier Middle Eastern experiences into fashion designs that appealed to a multitude of markets, Thea was able to continually relive and mine her memories, while still participating in an exciting modern life in the West. The rich combination of experience, a love of wonderful fabrics and above all, a passion not only for the Middle East itself but for that fantasy of the East evoked by her hero Poiret and others, have imbued her creations with a lasting appeal.

Left The Iraqi Samawa carpets incorporated figural human and animal designs alongside abstract patterns, and were ingeniously cut by Porter's dressmakers so that the motifs followed the lines of the coat. Cherie Federau collection.

Opposite Maudie James modelling a coat made from a Samawa carpet, trimmed with fur. It was popular with socialites including 'Baby Jane' Holzer. The design was adapted by Sandra Munro and made in chiffon. British *Vogue*, November 1970. Photograph by Barry Lategan.

Interior design

Thea Porter settled permanently in London in 1964 and sought to establish herself as an interior designer, which she began immediately by decorating friends' apartments with a mix of Western and Middle Eastern furniture. Staying at first with friends and family, she found work quickly with Elizabeth Eaton, an interior decorator known for creating traditional British interiors. However, she was asked to leave after a 'client warned Joy King (Eaton's real name) that Thea was recommending satin',[1] a textile far too extravagant and sensuous for Eaton's clientele. Following this debacle, for a short time she worked at Benny Gray's antique market off Oxford Street (he later opened both Alfie's and Gray's antiques markets in London). Porter now felt confident and knowledgeable enough to branch out on her own and was soon decorating grand residences with the same exotic palette she had first used for her friends. Thea's own style matched the emerging interest in Eastern decorative arts and interiors – satins included – that placed her at the forefront of a new trend in interiors, and ultimately, fashion too (p.65).

The uniqueness of Porter's life experience and personal style offered her novel ways in which to blend traditional Arabian craftsmanship with Orientalist taste, and apply this new aesthetic in modern European homes. She won a commission to work on the Syrian embassy in London,[2] as well as several private homes, such as the one belonging to the journalist Christopher Ward. Porter maximized the potential of his tiny flat using materials and colour (mostly beige, brown, black and white), combining out-sized Middle Eastern cushions and striped curtains for graphic effect – a transformation that she managed to deliver for only £300.[3]

london 1964–1974

The Story of Greek Street

Laura McLaws Helms

Banking on her own vision and sense of style, and intent on encouraging 'wider interests in the authentic styles and designs of Arabia',[4] Thea rented a first floor showroom on Berwick Street in London's Soho, in November 1965, selling imported furniture and decorative objects mostly from Syria. The shop was described at the time as being the ideal place to purchase the newly fashionable 'Arabian glamour for our own homes'.[5] Porter stocked 'mother-of-pearl furniture and ornaments from Damascus; embroidered Syrian table-cloths in sensuous blends of red, white and gold; magnificent Kurdish and Iraqi rugs; onyx and marble from Turkey and French-inspired fabrics from the Lebanon.'[6] The shop floor was layered and jumbled with decorative arts from all over the Middle East: furniture, textiles and *objets d'art* intermingled in a 'soukh-like setting of cushions and Middle Eastern ornaments.'[7] A lack of foot traffic led to the shop's closure after little over a month, although in that time, early customers included both model Talitha Getty (the Dutch wife of John Paul Getty, Jr, who bought an Egyptian hanging), and film director Stanley Donen (who purchased a Syrian mother-of-pearl mirror). Thea spent the next few months designing more interiors for personal clients before opening her iconic Greek Street shop on 27 July 1966, funded by two friends, Peter Kilner and Diana Wordsworth; together they were the first directors of Thea Porter Decorations, Ltd.[8]

Greek Street

Despite the fact that 8 Greek Street (a former Chinese restaurant) was 'boarded up and semi-derelict,' it was 'love ... at first sight' for Thea.[9] She liked 'the thought of Soho not only for its restaurants, strip clubs, prostitutes and reckless night life, but because there was no other shop there like the one I dreamed of creating, an exotic Aladdin's cave, full of baubles and pearly furniture, and hung with the rich fabrics I had collected in the East.'[10] Using these fabrics, seamstress Jean Tamboli made large cushions and curtains (as well as cravats) that would make their way from the shop into the homes of celebrities: Julie Christie ordered filmy velvet drapes.[11]

Contrary to the cool, minimalist, Mod Pop and Op Art-inspired interiors typical of the mid-1960s, Thea Porter Decorations tapped into a broader style that had moved away from a Western-focused sensibility. While *Time Magazine* hailed 'Swinging London',[12] and Carnaby Street was the centre of cool in 1966, the 'younger "bohemian" upper class, wealthy "international set" and new "classless" style setters'[13] were already looking for something new. Informed by the nineteenth- and early twentieth-century obsessions with the exotic, adventurous members of British high society ventured to Morocco or Afghanistan, bringing back with them 'de luxe exotic garments, often emphasizing their authenticity, antiquity and implied costliness'.[14] The hippie look started out as more of a political statement – a type of anti-fashion – but it soon became the fashion itself. The ragbag, ethnic aesthetic

Above Sketch for an early interior decoration project in London, about 1965.

OCT   69   •

thea porter orations

Above, clockwise from top left Thea outside her shop. Greek Street, London, October 1969.

Claudia Bruce outside

A model in the window of the shop. She wears a silk chiffon dress with the Samawa carpet print by Sandra Munro (p.59). Greek Street, London,

Left Moyra Swan in the Bahamas wearing a shirtdress made from Damascus tablecloth fabric known as *aghabani*. The shirtdress, in a variety of colours, became one of Porter's most successful designs and was produced in bulk at the Fortense factory. British *Vogue*, May 1969. Photograph by Arnaud de Rosnay.

Opposite Actress Fenella Fielding in a paisley *kaftan* on a matching Chesterfield couch in the shop. Photographs from this series ran in every major UK tabloid. Greek Street, London, October 1966. Photograph by William Lovelace.

of the hippie was easily copied and co-opted by others, including mass-market retailers: 'Soon everyone is going to be wearing *kaftans* – everyone, of course, being the sort of people who do their shopping in Carnaby-street.'[15]

This nascent stage of the hippie look helped usher in one of the great changes occurring in fashion production in the 1960s – the move towards pluralism in design, as heralded by Porter, which brought a greater variety of garment styles to the public than ever before. Porter was in a unique position – she could interpret authentically this Western fascination with Middle Eastern cultures, and hence offer chic Londoners an expertly curated, highly styled sampling of wearable traditional Middle Eastern heritage. As she explained: 'my shop almost immediately attracted rich hippies, actors, musicians and their women, who, rummaging excitedly through my fabrics, demanded that I make clothes for them.'[16]

67   London 1964–1974

Porter's first dress was a replica of a 'pretty little embroidered *kaftan* from Aleppo, a 14-year-old's wedding dress.'[17] Thea had discovered that she 'could use many of the same fabrics on women, chairs and walls. After all it is a form of upholstering, isn't it?'[18] Indeed, the first publicity photos for Thea Porter Decorations Ltd were of the actress Fenella Fielding kneeling on a coach upholstered in the same fabric as the *kaftan* she was wearing (p.67). These photographs went on to be printed in several daily newspapers – becoming the first of many times that celebrities would help Thea's designs gain recognition and sales. Beyond upholstery fabrics, Porter also found success producing a shirtdress made from embroidered tablecloths made in Damascus – photographed in British *Vogue* in 1969, they were one of the first designs to be produced in large numbers due to their popularity.

The unexpected flood of fashion commissions that followed this early publicity prompted Porter to stop working as an interior decorator and focus all of her attention on clothes. She was 'working at home at weekends, matching fabrics which has always been my passion and sketching designs almost by instinct, and then in the week struggling with pattern-makers, cutters and seamstresses to have them made.'[19] The Greek Street shop now offered bespoke design for male and female clients, in addition to the small number of ready-made Thea Porter designs (in limited sizes) on the rack (*opposite*).

Thea's designs were distinguished from the general aesthetic of the hippie movement by the high quality of the materials she used: antique fabrics and trimmings justified prices that ranged from around £100 to over £1,000 during this period. As well as Porter's own designs and antique pieces, her shop also became known for chokers with cascades of beads hanging down the front of the neck, made by a young jeweller, Bibette. These necklaces were modelled by Porter's assistant Claudia Bruce for *Nova*, and were worn by customers such as Swedish starlet Britt Ekland, who collected them in multiple colours.[20]

Menswear

Much of Porter's early fashion designs revolved around menswear, which conveniently appealed to those followers of rock and psychedelia. Two members of Pink Floyd wore her embellished jackets and printed shirts on the cover of their first album, *Piper at the Gates of Dawn*, released in August 1967 (p.70). The Beatles were her 'first big spenders'[21] when they came in to buy hangings, curtains and glass paintings to decorate their fashion and accessories shop, Apple Boutique (1967–8), in Baker Street. Prior to their visit to the Maharishi in India in February 1968, the band purchased shirts and jackets for themselves and sent their wives to be dressed in transparent clothes.[22] Mick Jagger, Brian Jones, Cat Stevens (Yusuf Islam) and Stuart Copeland (later of The Police) also ordered custom-made pieces. Jimi Hendrix even visited the shop a few days prior to his death and purchased

Left Roger Waters and Richard Right (at right) of Pink Floyd, dressed in Thea Porter to promote their first album, *Pipers at the Gates of Dawn*, 1967. Photograph by Vic Singh.

a peacock-print chiffon shirt: 'I remember he brought us an armful of carnations, so many that we couldn't find vases for them. He went out for a moment and returned with an empty Coca Cola can which he had picked up on the pavement, a half a dozen milk bottles which he filled with water and in which he tastefully arranged his flowers.'[23] Michael Butler, the producer of the hit Broadway musical *Hair*, was brought to the Greek Street shop in 1968 by his then-wife, Robin (who later married the banker Rupert Hambro in 1970 and became the London editor of American *Vogue*), and went on to order a jacket from Porter for every premiere of the show for the next few years.[24] Her extravagant men's designs (which included sumptuous dressing gowns and waistcoats of Damascus-brocaded silk) also found favour with the more eccentric members of the aristocracy: the Duke of Bedford wore her gilt-trimmed velvet tunics for country weekends at Woburn Abbey.[25]

The first shows

Porter showed her first official collection in a Lebanese restaurant on Kensington High Street on 28 June 1968. She was eager to expand the publicity and reach of her garments, and this first Caravanserai catwalk show (she later put on her shows as part of the London Designer Collections after they launched in 1975) allowed her to exhibit an enlarged fashion line to many more people than would normally travel to Greek Street.

The Caravanserai was 'a dark cavern of a place ideal for romantic diners.'[26] The collection was primarily composed of menswear (reflecting her clientele at that time), although Porter included some of her first full-length evening gowns as well as embroidered organdie mini-dresses. This show gained her the support of British *Vogue* and its fashion editor, Melanie Miller.[27] Under her tutelage, Porter designed the next two collections, which were shown at the Greek Street shop in December 1968 and Winter 1969: 'Feverishly, I assembled a far more daring and ambitious collection than anything I had done before, concentrating on evening clothes for women which were to remain my enduring interest.'[28]

On 2 December 1968, Porter showed a collection of 'exotic winter/ summer clothes' (p.72). Filled with editors, clients and friends, the small yet sumptuously decorated shop proved the ideal location to show the collection of brocade mini-dresses, cropped waistcoats, embroidered *kaftan*s and patterned velvet greatcoats. Following these successful shows, Porter's creations began to feature on the pages of British *Vogue*: the model Penelope Tree wore Porter's designs as a model, as well as in her personal life, as did her mother, the American socialite Marietta Tree; and prior to her tragic death in 1971, Talitha Getty picked up a butterfly-print robe to wear to the casino in Monaco as well as *kaftan*s for at-home wear in Morocco (p.74).

Right Printed on mirrored card, the invitation to Thea Porter's first fashion show in June 1968 included a hand of Fatima with the instruction: 'Press it out, keep it safe'. Design by Barney Bubbles and David Wills.
V&A: AAD/1995/4/20

Far right Thea used the protective Hand of Fatima again as the invitation to a show at the Greek Street shop in December 1968. It plays on Thea's own superstitious nature by incorporating a guide to palmistry.

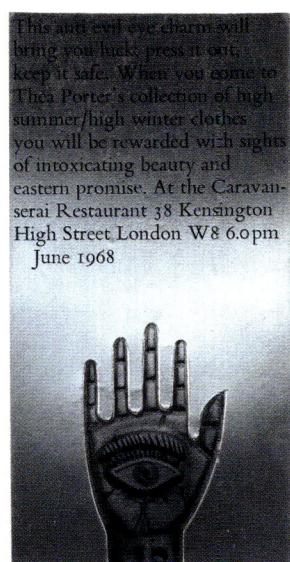

This anti evil eye charm will bring you luck, press it out, keep it safe. When you come to Thea Porter's collection of high summer/high winter clothes you will be rewarded with sights of intoxicating beauty and eastern promise. At the Caravanserai Restaurant 38 Kensington High Street London W8 6.0pm June 1968

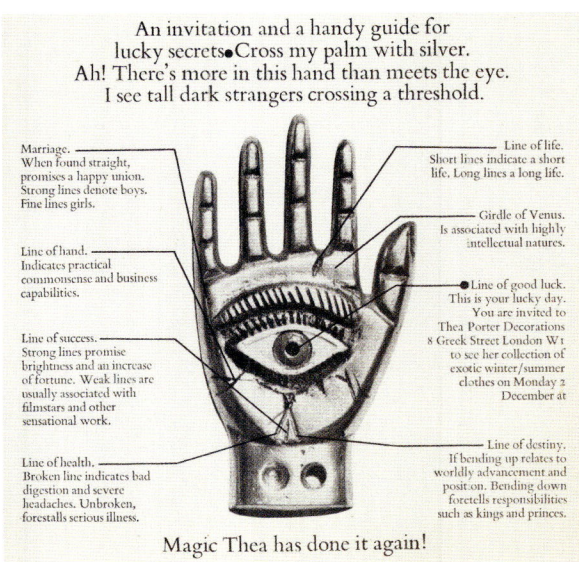

An invitation and a handy guide for lucky secrets●Cross my palm with silver. Ah! There's more in this hand than meets the eye. I see tall dark strangers crossing a threshold.

Marriage. When found straight, promises a happy union. Strong lines denote boys. Fine lines girls.

Line of hand. Indicates practical commonsense and business capabilities.

Line of success. Strong lines promise brightness and an increase of fortune. Weak lines are usually associated with filmstars and other sensational work.

Line of health. Broken line indicates bad digestion and severe headaches. Unbroken, forestalls serious illness.

Line of life. Short lines indicate a short life. Long lines a long life.

Girdle of Venus. Is associated with highly intellectual natures.

Line of good luck. This is your lucky day. You are invited to Thea Porter Decorations 8 Greek Street London W1 to see her collection of exotic winter/summer clothes on Monday 2 December at

Line of destiny. If bending up relates to worldly advancement and position. Bending down foretells responsibilities such as kings and princes.

Magic Thea has done it again!

Right, from top Marilyn Soames wearing a woven aluminium shirt at the first fashion show in the Caravanserai restaurant. London, June 1968.

Thea Porter's high summer/high winter 1968 show at the Caravanserai included this floor-length *lamé* waistcoat over a black satin dress.

The interior of Caravanserai reflected similar Middle Eastern motifs to those embroidered on the velvet waistcoat and skirt worn by the model.

Left, from top Thea Porter's second fashion show. This blue velvet coat was embroidered with a large geometric pattern and worn over a sheer blouse and wide-leg trousers. Greek Street, London, 2 December 1968.

An elaborately embroidered *kaftan* modelled at a fashion show at Thea Porter's Greek Street shop, 1968.

Mini-dress decorated with a psychedelic wave pattern, based on *ikat*, and *soutache* braid shown at Greek Street. London, 1968.

Left Chiffon dress shown in 1969. Inset waists and large abstract prints were common in Thea Porter's work. Greek Street, London, 1969.

Below Claudia Bruce wearing a peasant-style dress in a Persian paisley print combined with Damascus fabric, and a leather and feather headdress. Greek Street, London, 1969.

Left Maxi coat made from Sheila Hudson's Persian print, based on a design of Khosrow and Shirin playing polo found in Persian paintings and carpets of the 17th century and later (see pp.110–11). Fashion show at the Greek Street shop, London, 1969.

Left Emerald chiffon dress printed with Sheila Hudson's butterfly design. Talitha Getty wore this over green trousers to the Paris Casino for a night out with Rudolf Nureyev in 1970. V&A: T.347&A–1974

Below A page of Thea's sketches for dresses from the mid-1970s. Porter sketched her ideas quickly and then worked with her patternmakers to turn them into actual garments. V&A: AAD/1995/4/29

Art and fashion

Porter's knowledge of fashion production was limited by her background in art and design: 'In the beginning, I didn't know where fashion people bought fabrics, so I would buy Swiss voile and have it dyed to my specifications just as I did when I was decorating rooms.'[29] Speaking later of her lack of formal training as a fashion designer, she reflected: 'I wish I had started at Dior and learnt the trade, and had that kind of basic training … I can drape on a stand, know how a garment should fit and look, but I cannot sew or pattern cut. But seeing people dressed up every night gets your eye in.'[30] Yet Porter's artistic training in Beirut meant she was able to understand shape, colour and pattern: 'When I design a dress, I try to put it together like a painting: colours, shapes, proportions have to work together with the face, which is integral to the whole design. The dress must be a whole, have a certain necessity, in much the same way that a painting has a necessity of its own.'[31]

When Thea first started her company she mostly created custom-made pieces that did not require pattern grading. But as her off-the-rack market increased and her designs became more fitted, a different approach to producing the garments in various sizes became necessary. The process started with Thea sketching what long-time assistant Louise Fennell later described as 'these little rickety drawings':[32] though she was a trained artist, her sketches always had a naïve and seemingly half-finished sense to them, perfectly capturing the speed of her ideas and enthusiasms (*left*). Next, she would develop toiles (the industry term for a basic muslin garment pattern) with the aid of independently commissioned patternmakers. From 1968 to around 1979, Julian Yearwood ran a small factory (Fortense, owned by Ralph Forte and located on Charlotte Street most of the period) and worked with Thea as a patternmaker, producing the toiles for a number of key styles including the Faye, all the variations of the Gipsy and the shirtdresses.

Porter employed specialist outworkers to help her make different types of clothing in London, and relied on others for their expertise on the technical side of design.[33] Once she had a completed toile, it would be brought back to the shop, and according to Fennell, 'she was very engaged with it at that point. So if it came in and the waist was in the wrong place or anything was completely wrong, she would pull it off and re-pin it again. She knew absolutely what she wanted.'[34] Meg Lake, her first seamstress in the late 1960s who returned to work for Thea again around 1972, remembers Porter as being hands-on and collaborative in all aspects of design and production. The same approach continued as recalled by Carla Codara, who worked for Thea Porter for eight years (c.1980–6): 'She was very good at involving you in [the design], which is something that I'd never done before because I was working in a factory, and you're not really supposed to give your opinion about things. But she made you feel like you were part of the process.'[35]

As a next step, Porter would send the outworkers off with a combination of fabrics that she had chosen, from which samples were made up of each design. Once customers had decided what pieces they wanted to order, they would be measured and Thea would choose the selection of fabrics and trims that would be used for each garment, paying close attention to what she thought would emphasize the beauty of the wearer (therefore no two pieces were exactly the same, as she liked to combine the fabrics in an almost instinctive manner according to the customer). Julian Yearwood cut the fabric (in very small runs) for many different styles, which was then passed on to the outworkers. Orders were paid for, half in advance, and the other half on completion. By replicating the Parisian couture salon experience in this way, Porter provided a comfortable setting for her clientele and differentiated herself from her contemporaries in London, who primarily relied on ready-to-wear sales.

Colour and pattern

Porter's highly sophisticated sense of colour was the result of considerable contemplation. According to Louise Fennell: 'She'd often just put different bits of material on the floor and ... looked at them, and moved them about a bit; tried different things with different things before they even went near the outworkers who were making them up into dresses. So she arranged each one in its way – sometimes you thought, "Ooo, really??" but it always worked brilliantly.'[36]

At the back of the shop behind a screen was Thea's office and workroom (*opposite*), with a cupboard where she kept a wide array of textiles and trims. Venetia Porter also remembers that her mother 'would have drawers she'd open up which contained antique fabrics or bits of sari. It was literally pulling things out and putting them on the fabric. She'd always hold the fabric up to her, so quite often – she'd look at it in the mirror to see how did it look on her first ... She would pick up these little pieces and start to put them together.'[37] Though the colours and textures might clash, the mix of fabrics was never disharmonious. For Porter, fashion was about bringing art and pattern to life: 'Modern life is rooted in new sounds, new rhythms, new pace, tempo, pulse beats. Never in history have these been so fast changing. A preference for clothes that play with colour and pattern [is] today's response to today's rhythms. Pattern is the most compelling force in fashion today and that will not change for a long time.'[38]

Fabrics and textiles

Unable to find textiles that were unique and exotic enough for her fantastical garments, even quite early in her career as a designer, Porter began to have textiles designed exclusively for her company. The collaborative process was key: she would often draft a sketch, or give the textile designer something to inspire or adapt that was then translated into a pattern and then cloth.

77　London 1964–1974

Below left Dancer Rudolf Nureyev modelling a scarf in Sandra Munro's print of patchwork squares. British *Vogue*, June 1972. Photograph by Cecil Beaton.

Below right Chiffon pattern of patchwork squares by Sandra Munro. It was based on a design from her degree collection at the Glasgow School of Art in 1969.

Right Peacock print by Sandra Munro, inspired by Aubrey Beardsley. Although Munro confessed to never being happy with how this design turned out, the print, here in velvet, was reproduced in a range of different fabrics and became one of Thea Porter's signature styles.

Opposite Printed pleated chiffon cape. Included in the Cecil Beaton exhibition *Fashion: An Anthology* at the Victoria and Albert Museum, London, 1971. V&A: T.344&A–1974

These designers included Katharine Hamnett (b.1947; the fashion designer who designed textiles for Porter while she was still a student at Central Saint Martins, producing new paisley prints in the late 1960s for some of Porter's earliest designs), and Sandra Munro (b.1948), who produced Porter's most famous textile in 1968 – the 'Peacock' print.[39] Munro met Porter when she graduated from art school in Glasgow and won a competition that allowed her to show her degree collection in London. At the time, Munro was working on designs that created patchworks out of multiple sections of intricate patterns, which immediately captured Thea's attention (*previous pages*). She ordered designs from the degree selection and commissioned Munro to create many more over subsequent years, including a landscape print based on the work of Lebanese painter, Khalil Zgheib (1911–75, see p.22), and a print of swirling arabesques of attenuated peacocks. Printed in black against a rainbow of different colours, this print is a modern reworking of illustrations by Aubrey Beardsley (1872–98).[40] Porter would have been conscious of the appearance of peacocks in many different cultures, having visited the Peacock throne-room in the Shah's palace in Tehran while on a diplomatic trip with her husband in the early 1960s.[41]

The decadent look of the peacock print meant that it was well-suited for a number of different purposes: as voile curtains in Porter's mirrored dining room or covering her inlaid mother-of-pearl Syrian chairs;[42] at the Greek Street shop, at one time, as a 'peacock-printed calico curtain' which separated the shop from office and workshop areas;[43] and as shirts in Porter's first Caravanserai collection – 'some black-and-white, peacock-printed shirts for men in see-through chiffon, a shade dandified perhaps, but not in the least outrageous.'[44] In her Spring 1970 collection, Porter unveiled a 'three-tier, sunburst-pleated evening cape, showing a group of strutting peacocks in black and white.'[45] It was this piece that Cecil Beaton chose for his exhibition of 'milestones in fashion',[46] *Fashion: An Anthology*, at the V&A Museum in October 1971 (p.78).

Thea met the textile designer Janet Taylor at a design fair in around 1969, and they worked together for over 20 years. Lilies were Thea's favourite flower, and as she described in her memoir: 'Janet Taylor printed some wonderful lilies for me, and again, they went on and on for years, she embellished the print with hand painting – it was a great success: there were at least six variations of the lilies in different colourways; she then printed lilies on calico for my blinds' (p.82).[47] Unlike the swirling forms of the 'Peacock' print, the 'Lily' (created in 1971, the same year Zandra Rhodes created a collection of prints also based on lilies) was a more graphic, Art Deco-style print.[48]

Some of Taylor's designs, such as her abstract skyscraper print (*opposite*), were engineered for particular garments: she was given the pattern pieces and would then lay out the textile design to perfectly fit perfectly. In many

Right Maudie James modelling a multi-layered silk chiffon skyscraper print dress in 1970. Adapted from a design from her graduation collection, Janet Taylor's Art Deco-inspired skyscraper print appeared on velvets, silks and chiffons. Photograph by Patrick Hunt.

ways, large-scale abstract patterns suited the flowing and voluminous shapes of many of Porter's garments. A 'Butterfly' print by Sheila Hudson[49] is a close-up field of overlapping butterfly wings, the delicate black tracing of the wings was printed on backgrounds of different colours and fabrics, lending an ethereal effect to her designs. According to Porter, one could 'never tire of it because it was just wings with the texture and the magical pattern';[50] the print was used on a number of different garment styles including Gipsy dresses and robes, as worn by Joan and Jackie Collins in 1970. Other large-scale patterns were hand-painted by the artist Hannah Meckler including swirling waves,[51] cascades of hearts and marble effects, all painted on to metres of silk chiffon that were made into evening dresses and *abayas*. Using Batik techniques Meckler also produced fabrics with graphic Oriental-style flowers used for gipsy dresses and other garments.

Ikats, the patterned textiles that result from resist-dyeing yarn prior to weaving,[52] are found in cultures all over the non-Western world, from the Middle East to India and Indonesia, and were a favourite of Thea's: 'in the Sixties the hippies brought back beautiful *ikats* from Turkestan and India, and they were pink and red and green, and very exciting.'[53] Sheila Hudson would create several pseudo-*ikats* for Porter, which were printed on cottons, satins, chiffons and velvets, and then sometimes completely beaded too, producing a stunning shimmering effect. Even Thea's brother Patrick was married in a suit made of one of these pseudo-*ikats* in 1972

Below left Lily print on satin, by Janet Taylor for Thea Porter in the mid-1970s. Lilies were Porter's favourite flower, and the print was used extensively on garments and furnishings. V&A: AAD/1995/4/16

Below right Angela White wearing a black-and-gold leopard-print halter top and a hobble fronted skirt in the Greek Street shop at the launch of the Spring/Summer 1981 collection. Janet Taylor's lily print on calico is in the background. London, 1981. Press Association Archive.

Right Handpainted colourways of the butterfly print, produced by Sheila Hudson for Spring/Summer 1970.
V&A: AAD/1995/4/16

Below Joan Collins in a Gipsy dress, with her sister Jackie in a robe with trailing sleeves over trousers, in two versions of Sheila Hudson's butterfly print, at the opening of the musical *1776* in 1970.

Left Hannah Meckler created hand-painted fabrics inspired by marbling techniques that were particularly well-suited to Thea Porter's *abayas*. 1977. Cherie Federau collection.

Below Hand-painted chiffon by Hannah Meckler. Meckler's fabrics, evoking waves and clouds, were often used on *abayas* and other garments.

Right Thea's brother
Patrick at his wedding
to Lamorna Heath,
10 March 1972. Both
dressed by Thea;
Patrick's suit was made
of *ikat* fabric. London.
Photograph by
Sophie Baker.

(*above*).[54] Porter's Spring 1972 collection also included a series of prints
designed by Munro, inspired by Buddhist imagery that appeared on the wall
paintings of Dunhuang on the silk route and elsewhere (p.86) and intricately
stacked pagodas that appeared on silk pyjamas and wool blouses. Porter also
collaborated with the Hungarian textile designer Michael Szell (1930–2002),
who had a life-long passion for the Middle East. A frequent visitor to Iran
as a child, his passion for Persian carpets and art developed into a career
designing furnishing fabrics.[55] Porter had used his work in her interior
designs, and loved his formal Islamic patterns; she asked him to print them
on silk for her in 1971 and the resulting fabrics evoked the designs of Persian
fabrics and tiles, the thin silks rippling with traditional arabesques, stars
and floral motifs on an enormous scale. Szell also designed a series of linear,
one-colour paisley prints that were included in her 1969 collection (p.90).[56]

Porter enjoyed finding and using novel textiles in her clothes; her good
friend Jutta Laing once described Porter as 'courageous' in her fabric choices
after she cut up a beautiful antique patterned shawl to make Jutta a pair of
trousers.[57] Although she was criticized for her use of valuable textiles, Porter
responded: '… to have a shimmering piece of exquisite silk near the face is
so enhancing, and anyway, if you keep antique silks in a bag some of them
will rot away.'[58] The antique fabrics and trims that she bought from special
dealers were such an integral part of the look she had cultivated, that it was
difficult for Porter to move away from them.[59] Beyond this, her well-heeled

clients were more than willing to pay for these one-of-a-kind details that added a sense of value and uniqueness to a Thea Porter design.

In May of 1971, the same month Porter would open her New York shop (see p.102), an agreement was reached with French manufacturer Bernard Frères Ltd to produce a ready-to-wear line. This new Thea Porter collection would use many of the same patterns and textile designs as her couture line, but would be produced more cheaply. It was launched in October of that year and was sold in shops nationwide, including Miss Selfridge. The majority of the designs were of thin cotton voile, but the collection also included several variations of the now-iconic Gipsy dress, made from red and black floral Liberty prints (p.91). In contrast to the elegant simplicity of the lowercase sans serif used on her couture labels (*opposite*), the label for these ready-to-wear pieces featured Porter's name next to a hand-drawn flower, a nod to the mass-market's interest in hippie culture. According to Porter, the pieces were to be priced at around £40 each, but the contract with Bernard Frères Ltd was terminated in May 1972 following discovery that they

Above left Sandra Munro's 'Buddha' print in chiffon, 1972.

Above right A smocked tunic and trousers, both in satin with a print based on a Buddhist wall painting designed by Sandra Munro for Autumn/Winter 1972. *Country Life*, August 1972. **Photograph by Christopher Moore.**

Below Porter used a simple lowercase sans serif script for her labels, 'thea porter couture' or 'thea porter london' for more than two decades.

The label for Thea Porter's short-lived ready-to-wear line in 1971 bowed to lingering hippie tastes.

were being sold at around £75 per piece and therefore priced in more direct competition with her couture line.[60]

The highs of 1971 (opening an international outpost and launching another line) were tempered by the failure of both within a year. Regardless of these setbacks, Porter forged ahead, continuing to create and push her fantasies into new ground and sharing the Clothing Institute's Designer of the Year award with Zandra Rhodes in December 1972.[61] She also began a successful partnership with Elizabeth Arden, selling one-of-a-kind garments in Arden's Bond Street shop. Launched with a fashion show at the boutique, the seating of Princess Margaret in the front row led to a front-page story in *Women's Wear Daily* that proclaimed Porter's designs to have an 'Easy Elegance, the kind of clothes to slip into when you've had your hair done and have $500 burning a hole in your Hermes bag.'[62] After this first meeting, Princess Margaret had a number of garments made for her by Thea – the sparkling, heavily embellished tops and gowns were well-suited for the constant round of events and galas she attended.

Left Faye dress in *ikat* silk chiffon, designed by Sandra Munro, with a bodice of Damascus brocade. Cherie Federau collection.

Opposite Anne Schaufuss in a long antique *ikat* tunic over a chiffon *ikat* blouse and velvet knickerbockers. The setting sun effect was made by rephotographing two colour transparencies layered over each other. British *Vogue*, December 1970. Photograph by Clive Arrowsmith.

Below Scarlet wedding dress, 1972. Porter chose a heavily embroidered scarlet sari to make the wedding dress of her good friend Jutta when she married the psychiatrist R.D. Laing; red is the traditional colour of bridal garments in India. Jutta Laing collection.

Below right Dress made from a Michael Szell fabric of black chiffon, with stylized paisley design in white, 1969. Made for Thea's university friend Jacqueline Bullen. Venetia Porter collection.

Opposite Gipsy dress in a Liberty print cotton voile, part of the ready-to-wear collection Autumn/Winter 1971. The keyhole was stitched closed, but was opened by a later owner to allow for more of a *décolloté*. Liz Goldwyn collection. Photograph by Amanda Charchian.

Clientele

Porter did not always come out from her studio for every customer, but for the most glamorous and beautiful she would, 'rush up and down the stairs a dozen times, unfurling rolls of fabric until the basement was a sea of pale satin, tremulous chiffon and foamy lace, edged with trimming and beading – a stormy sea out of which I would seek to magic up a dress or two'.[63]

Her main clients continued to visit the Greek Street shop, keen for Porter's personal attention. Lady Annabel Goldsmith (then Birley), the high society hostess and muse behind the famous London club, Annabel's, recalls how Porter would make everything for her extremely low-cut, which infuriated her then-lover (and later husband) James Goldsmith (who would joke: 'Thea is my enemy').[64] She made all of Lady Goldsmith's evening clothes, and one spangled gown in particular, featured in a portrait sitting with the other directors of Annabel's, reinforcing the transcendence of Porter's designs from their hippie beginnings to the top level of London society. Another client from 1969 was Baroness Rawlings who bought many dresses. She recalled that 'they were original, glamorous, easy to wear' and that 'Thea was very special and had adorable assistants.'[65]

With clothes that were described by *Country Life* as 'spectacular in a theatrical sort of way, but [which] look ravishing on the right people',[66] it is unsurprising that Porter's designs found their way into the wardrobes of intriguing and exotic personalities. She recalls in her memoir how: 'A tall impeccably dressed man in a double-breasted chalk-stripe ordered an extravagant evening gown to his own measurements: it was Barry Humphries, the creator of the outrageous Dame Edna. As he explained in an interview with David Taylor of *Sunday Times Magazine,* "In the old days, when Edna was rather more frumpish, I'd just buy her a kit from department stores." He added, however, that when Edna became more stylish, he used to repair "to Thea Porter in Greek Street, where Edna's extra-specially stunning outfits are generally run up."'[67]

The transsexual model April Ashley, whose divorce from a peer made her the 'most talked about personality' in the 1970s,[68] adored Porter's designs and often wore a calf-length, beaded fringe silk crop top, with nothing underneath (the top was originally shown with matching harem trousers). It was these looks, inspired by exotic belly dancers among other cultural niceties of the time, that caused Marylou Luther, the *Los Angeles Times* fashion editor, to name Porter the 'mother of the "Rich Hippie" look':[69] 'It's all for and about the over-privileged set. It's the Establishment playing anti-Establishment fashion ... You take the best of the hippie happenings you see every day on the street ... But instead of scrounging them from thrift shops and steamer trunks, you buy them from a new breed of designers such as England's Thea Porter and Jean Muir. And you pay. You really pay.'[70]

Above Sketch for a wedding dress for the socialite, interior designer and sister of the Duchess of Cornwall, Annabel Shand. Shand married Simon Elliot in April 1972 in a Faye dress with lace *appliqué* on the bodice, sleeves and a scalloped skirt train.

A number of clients from the Middle East ordered Thea's clothes. Mrs Nadia Adham from Saudi Arabia, for whom Thea made numerous *abayas*, would remark that 'Thea's clothes could span any period from Haroun al-Rashid to the present day'.[71] She was also popular among Iranian women in the court of the Empress Farah Pahlavi, who would buy quantities of them,[72] while the Empress herself also had some garments made for her. Channelling this clientele, 'treasures from Thea Porter's new age of splendour' were photographed for British *Vogue* inside the ornately inlaid and carved interiors of the nineteenth-century Golestan Palace in Tehran.[73]

Swinging London

London was the centre of Thea's life and career: although she travelled and sold her designs internationally, her work became permanently linked to her adoptive city. Her social and business world centred around the Greek Street shop and her nearby home in Bolton Street, but alongside that, Porter developed a lifestyle that crossed various strata of society and incorporated people from diverse cultural worlds.

A 'disorderly array of beauty',[74] the shop was the locus of Thea's world from which she set out on Saturdays to stock up on books about art and fashion in bookshops such as Zwemmer's on Charing Cross Road. She would sometimes leave the shop in the afternoons and venture over to the legendary Colony Room Club on nearby Dean Street, where she interacted with a world totally outside that of fashion and high society. The Club was a sanctuary where Porter could indulge in her love of art, conversation and a good drink: 'Presided over

Below left Among many royal clients was the Iranian Empress Farah Pahlavi, who wore a Porter silk *abaya* for this official portrait.

Below right Lauren Hutton in a gold velvet shirtdress with heavy gold tasselled buttons. Golestan Palace, Tehran. British *Vogue*, December 1969. Photograph by Henry Clarke.

by the foul mouthed but golden hearted Muriel Belcher, and her partner Ian Board (known as Ian Board-stiff), this afternoon drinking club attracted such patrons as the painters Lucien Freud and Francis Bacon, the jazz-playing writer and collector George Melly and a host of other talented, if somewhat inebriate, friends ... No one ever left the Colony sober.' [75]

Home life

Thea's home on Bolton Street in Mayfair exuded a heady and exotic atmosphere: *The first impression of her flat is already of a knockout richness. Parts of it are like a gorgeous tent, with big patterns sprawling over the low ceilings of the bedrooms. The second impression is of intricate workmanship – the number of foreign objects beautifully inlaid or embroidered and the way English craftsmen, for Thea Porter, have carpeted and papered and braided and finished to match.* [76]

Most vividly expressing Thea's 'passion for pattern' was her bedroom, completely papered with large-scale green-and-red poppies on a black ground ('I love to feel I'm weaving through poppies'),[77] and with an ornate mirrored headboard over a brightly coloured Indian patchwork bedspread. The L-shaped living room, which she designed in 1970, had black carpeting, a silver ceiling, a Damascus inlaid mother-of-pearl chest, black suede sofa and walls covered with a specially woven copy of a 1910 French fabric in black, silver and gold. The dining alcove was a 'dazzling dreamlike world where everybody is reflected a thousand bewildering times between mirror tables,

Below left Thea Porter's bedroom, decorated with Coles wallpaper. One of her own paintings hangs next to the bed. Photograph by Oberto Gili. V&A: AAD/1995/4/1

Below right Andrew Logan's seven-foot silver lily sculpture in Porter's black-and-silver Art Deco inspired living room. Photograph by Oberto Gili. V&A: AAD/1995/4/1

Opposite Thea Porter reflected in the mirrored dining room table at her flat in Bolton Street, Mayfair. *Sunday Times*, 7 March, 1971. Photograph by Jim Lee.

mirror ceiling, and walls, while the silver metal blinds and woven aluminium curtains add to the fantasy'.[78] (The curtains were later changed to gauze printed with her 'Peacock' pattern, p.78.)

A chance encounter with the young artist Andrew Logan (b.1945) at an Institute of Contemporary Arts exhibition in 1970 provided Thea with the role of patron. Highly struck by Logan's giant flowers, Porter commissioned him to build for her living room a tall silver lamp with a large lily-shaped shade – the bulb was encased in the gold stamen and an amoeba-like black cushion around the base allowed her to sit below it. When describing her ideal Sunday for the *Telegraph* in 1977, Thea wrote of her mornings: 'I have time to carry [Turkish coffee] through to the mirror dining room table which reflects and holds whatever light there is. I enjoy the calm pool of reflected lilies and mother of pearl.'[79] After a bath she would return: 'At last, my hair blown dry, with sketching pads, thin and thick pens, I sit under my Andrew Logan lily feeling rather like the caterpillar in *Alice in Wonderland* who is sitting on a fly agaric mushroom, which grows wild in the English countryside and which has hallucinogenic properties.'[80] At a later date the lily was moved to the Greek Street shop – Logan then constructed two intertwining palm trees with dangling, lit-up mirrored hearts for Thea's home.

A loyal team

There was always a band of steadfast and devoted workers helping Thea in the Greek Street shop. From the early interior design days, she was assisted by Reg Butcher who ran errands and made repairs on the run-down shop. Counter-balancing his gruff appearance were a string of glamorous shop girls who worked as *vendeuses* and managed the accounts. Fran Yorke who worked for her in 1968 described herself as 'a glorified dogsbody; sewing, serving, shopping, driving, but also invited to join in some quite exciting events, usually wearing something delicious borrowed from the racks.'[81] Claudia Bruce worked in the shop from 1968 until 1971, and later brought her flatmate, Boo Brassey, in to join her in running the shop around 1970. The dawn of the 1970s brought with it even greater success for Porter's designs, yet the business side of the company was often left in the control of young girls more skilled at modelling and selling than book-keeping.

Noteworthy employees included Frenchman Bruno Mossa, who dealt primarily with the clients and sales, and went on to help open Thea's New York shop; Mossa's friend, Laurent Marcel, who assisted with Porter's shows as early as 1970 and then worked closely with her from 1972 until the end of the decade, helping with the measuring of customers and ordering of garments; Emma Chetwode, who was described by the gossip columnists as 'the lovely nineteen-year old niece of the Earl of Minto';[82] Fiona Dunlop (who briefly worked at Greek Street in 1977 before relocating to Paris to manage the shop there later that year); an Australian former model Lynn

Below Fiona Dunlop, Louise Fennell and Lynn Richardson at work in the Greek Street shop, 1976. Photograph by Alberto Salvagno.

Richmond; and most notably Louise Fennell, who assisted Thea for a number of years from 1974 until the closure of the shop in 1981 (*below*):

My first real job was found for me by accident, somewhere amidst the smoke and booze soaked crowd at the infamous Colony Room Club, in Soho in 1974. My uncle, a frequent habitué, found himself chatting to a woman called Thea Porter, she was perched on a bar stool next to Francis Bacon. Thea told him she desperately needed someone to work in her dress shop in Greek Street; he said he had a niece interested in fashion ... so I was told to report there the following Monday. No interview, no references, no employment contract or talk of wages; just go there and start. I arrived at 10am, as instructed, to find another girl, small, blonde and efficient looking, who was also there to try out for the same job. My heart sank. We were told to tidy shelves until Thea arrived to inspect us. I don't remember whether she spoke to us at all but, tiny though she was, she made quite an impact; she went into a spectacular meltdown over a dress that had arrived from an outworker and was not up to scratch. It was a formidable performance; the next day the other prospective shop-girl failed to show and the job was mine. I couldn't quite believe my luck.[83]

Porter had built a group of artistic, like-minded people around her: many of her assistants also modelled her designs, while various professional models became good friends and walked in her shows. The American model Jan Ward met Porter in 1974, and began modelling for her prior to her marriage to photographer (and Twiggy impresario) Justin de Villeneuve in 1975. Hazel Collins worked with Thea for over ten years, appearing in catwalk shows and publicity photos until 1984. Often the models would be paid for their time with garments – de Villeneuve recalls: 'I didn't get any money but I got clothes, and that was fantastic. Thea gave me some beautiful things.'[84]

By working with friends, Porter kept costs down and was also able to support their artistic endeavours: for a show in 1972, the artist Penny Slinger both modelled and created bridal masks of feathers and pearls (*opposite*); Andrew Logan was brought in to design mirrored jewellery for several collections in the early 1970s; while Van Pariser, a beauty and fashion photographer, shot most of the in-house promotional imagery used by Porter in the mid-to-late-1970s. Porter would give him the clothes and he would choose the model and the location, and he often borrowed her designs to use for advertising shoots. She never paid him for his photos – everything was done on a friendly basis, with both helping each other's careers. Many of the shop assistants, collaborators and outworkers continued to work for her for many years; Jean Tamboli, for example, produced cushions for Porter from 1966 until the end of her career.

An expanding business

Among the high points of the early 1970s were two shows Thea put on at the London nightclub Tramps. For 'Wild Winter Flowers', her Autumn/ Winter 1970 collection, shown in June, all the ensembles were named after flowers (opening with 'Acanthus', a Liberty wool paisley dress trimmed in

Below left The invitation to the Autumn/Winter 1970 show 'Wild Winter Flowers' overlays the protective Hand of Fatima with a motif from a Central Asian *suzani* textile. V&A: AAD/1995/4/22

Below right Thea's friend Jutta Laing often collaborated with her, including illustrating the programme for Porter's Spring 1974 show, held at Elizabeth Arden's Bond Street shop. V&A: AAD/1995/4/10

Opposite Thea was a great admirer of the tailor Tommy Nutter. His striped suit was shown alongside Porter's white eyelet bridal gown and mask, made by Penny Slinger, as the perfect wedding ensemble. *Country Life*, 19 April 1973. Photograph by Christopher Moore.

Above Two models in Thea Porter onstage at Modefest. Trogir (former Yugoslavia), 1973.

red snakeskin (bought by 'Baby Jane' Holzer and now in the collection of the Metropolitan Museum of Art in New York) and closing with 'Sesamum' (a brocade fox-trimmed coat). Two years later Porter showed another collection at Tramps on 13 June 1972 – an auspicious date chosen by a fortune-teller. She received a telegram from close friend Edna O'Brien on the eve of the show, it read: 'DARLING THEA JAMES JOYCE DID ALL HIS MAJOR THINGS ON THE 13TH SO YOU SEE IT WILL BE A LUCKY DAY LOVE EDNA.'[85] In 1973, she began her successful partnership with Elizabeth Arden, selling one-of-a-kind garments in Arden's Bond Street shop (p.87). For her spring 1975 collection, Porter moved the setting to the elegant Crush Bar at the Royal Opera House in London.

The growing renown of London's fashion industry provided Thea and her contemporaries with opportunities to exhibit their designs abroad (*above*). In 1974 she was sent as an envoy for British fashion along with Bill Gibb to Modefest, a weeklong summer festival held at Trogir in former Yugoslavia (now Croatia).[86] The previous April Thea took part in 'Designs on Fashion', a group showing organized by the British Overseas Trade Council. Her outfits were modelled alongside those of Mary Quant (b.1934), Ossie Clark, Bill Gibb, Zandra Rhodes, John Bates (b.1938), Tim Gardner, Gina Fratini, Jean Muir (1928–1995) and Alice Pollock (b.1942) (*opposite*).[87]

Designs on Fashion

John Bates Ossie Clark Gina Fratini Tim Gardner Bill Gibb Jean Muir Alice Pollock Thea Porter Mary Quant Zandra Rhodes

Vogue

Thea Porter's association with British *Vogue*, honed since she set up shop in London, proved an invaluable introduction on her first trip to New York in the summer of 1968. Though quite shy herself, her fans already included socialites and starlets in London who wore her clothes as they jet-setted around the world. Porter flew to New York with a suitcase stuffed with clothes and an introduction from Melanie Miller to Diana Vreeland, the editor-in-chief of American *Vogue* and the era's undisputed arbiter of American fashion. As Thea would later recount:

A wonderful thing then happened. I was no sooner settled in at the Algonquin, the celebrated hotel at 59 West 44th Street, which was to be for many years my American headquarters, than I was visited by no less a person than the great Diana Vreeland ... Accompanied by a bevy of her fashion editors, lean and elegant as only American women can be, Mrs Vreeland swept imperially into my suite, sternly examined a rail or two of my diaphanous creations, and pronounced herself pleased. I was made.[1]

Vreeland understood Thea's ideal clientele instantly and organized for Carrie Donovan, American *Vogue*'s fashion editor, to bring 'Baby Jane' Holzer, the Warhol star and New York society darling, to the Algonquin Hotel. Immediately enamoured with the outlandish clothes that matched

new york 1968–1971

American expansion   *Laura McLaws Helms*

Left Socialite and Warhol Superstar 'Baby Jane' Holzer modelled this aluminium shirt and waistcoat for the first appearance of Thea Porter clothes in American *Vogue*, 4 November 1968. Photograph by Hogenboom.

her outrageous lifestyle, Holzer was photographed for American *Vogue* wearing a see-through chiffon blouse as well as an aluminium top and metal chain-embellished waistcoat (*above*).[2] These pieces were all available at Henri Bendel, the high-end Manhattan women's shop whose president, Geraldine Stutz, had an intuitive eye for new fashion talent (several years later she was the first client of American fashion designer Mary McFadden (b.1938; see p.29 – her African-made *kaftans* were an alternative approach to the Western quest for the exotic).

Wholesale

Henri Bendel was Thea's first wholesale client – up until this point, all sales had taken place at her Greek Street shop. Bendel's original order was not without issue: six outfits were commissioned, and each one produced with a different lining; Bendel's wired to say they must all be made the same. Regardless of this, Stutz agreed to open a Thea Porter shop within 'The Fancy' – Bendel's more youth-conscious floor, which also included a mini Jean Muir shop. Replicating the feel of Porter's Greek Street headquarters, the shop was opened at the beginning of November 1969. *Women's Wear Daily* described it immediately: 'the Bendel Shop has it all – including the medieval Persian prints hung on the walls, the ornamented pillows, the Porter-printed muslin on the walls and David Hicks tile-patterned carpet on the floor. And on the rails – "a little of everything" – the slender, gold-braided caftans to antique belt over chiffon trousers, high-waisted, side-slit caftans in silk-braid-bound tapestries, medieval dresses, and "dozens and dozens" of gipsy dresses in velvet and patterned gauze or in velvet and French-ribbon-patched chiffon to wear with flying turbans and velvet boots.'[3]

Bendel's chic 57th street location combined with Stutz's novel approach to fashion retailing had made the shop the locus of shopping activity for all rich yet hip socialites, who began purchasing Thea's designs to wear to galas and other glamorous events. The first customer on the morning it opened was Jacqueline Kennedy Onassis who purchased three items;[4] many of Porter's other jet-set clients (including actresses Julie Christie and Joanne Woodward) supplemented their wardrobes there in between visits to Greek Street. The boutique within Bendel's closed several months later after Porter unknowingly broke her exclusivity agreement by agreeing to sell to Bloomingdale's as well. However, in the long run, the Bloomingdale's relationship brought with it the opportunity to sell to more retail outlets across America.

Pop and celebrity culture

With Thea Porter designs now firmly ensconced in the wardrobes of the best-dressed women in New York, and on the racks of internationally celebrated retail boutiques, success seemed inevitable. In 1967, Jenny Fabian and Johnny Byrne referred to her designs in their controversial novel *Groupie*. 'I don't care what you do to me,' Jenny's heroine exclaimed, 'but please don't harm my Thea Porter trousers'. Jenny herself had purchased embroidered black and gold trousers at the Greek Street shop in 1968,[5] and the experience would shape the book's 19-year-old protagonist Katie, who vividly described how she 'blew a lot of bread at Thea Porter's, my favourite shop as yet undiscovered by too many people.'[6] Other literary references to Porter's designs included Judith Krantz's 1978 blockbuster, *Scruples*.[7] Porter and her designs had thus become firmly enmeshed into the fabric of contemporary pop culture.

Left This combination of a sheer gold *lamé* top with trousers and waistcoat in an intricate frond pattern exemplifies Porter's ability to make unconventional textile combinations. Cherie Federau collection.

Opposite Maudie James modelling a long tunic over matching trousers in hand-painted velvet. British *Vogue*, October 1969. Photograph by Guy Bourdin.

'Mrs Vreeland swept imperially into my suite, sternly examined a rail or two of my diaphanous creations, and pronounced herself pleased. I was made.'

The sense of discovering a private secret known to only the most fashion-forward and far out helped to create a particular and devoted clientele, but this was lost by the end of the decade as the 'Thea Porter' name became increasingly recognized beyond the world of stylish London. Her connection to the worlds of cinema and music began to to be increasingly enhanced as celebrities started to appear regularly in the tabloids dressed in her exotic ensembles. International royalty also had a taste for Porter's clothes: the Empress of Iran Farah Pahlavi (p.93), Begum Aga Khan (Sarah Croker-Poole) and Princess Grace of Monaco (the American film star, Grace Kelly) were all ordering exclusive Thea Porter designs to adorn their private and public lives.

Thea Porter New York

Due to the strength of her clientele in New York, Thea set out to expand her business there by opening a shop (*opposite*), and looked to Michael Butler (p.70), the impresario behind the rock musical *Hair*, to back it since he wore Porter's designs for all special events. At the time, he described Porter's designs as 'the ultimate in female dramatics, Scheherazade up in lights.'[8] With his vast personal wealth and love of her clothes, he let two floors of a brownstone townhouse at 203 East 60th Street to open Thea Porter New York, which was to sell 'furniture, cushions and antique hangings as well as clothes, doffing our cap to the notion of "total taste".'[9]

The shop opened on 17 May 1971 (an auspicious date chosen by Butler's astrologer), with a ground floor shop and a wholesale showroom above. It was decorated as an Art Deco version of Arabian Nights, with black, silver and gold fabric draped on the walls and giant cushions strewn on the floor.[10] With the press handled by Eleanor Lambert (the doyenne of American fashion PR and the founder of the Council of Fashion Designers of America), the launch drew considerable crowds, eager to sample the latest fashion from London. The 'eye-popping mixture of the beautiful and bizarre people'[11] included Peter Yarrow (of the American folk singing trio Peter, Paul & Mary),

'Baby Jane' Holzer, actress Julie Newmar, journalist Lally Weymouth, socialite Nan Kempner, Sam Newhouse (the owner of Condé Nast), Andy Warhol with a retinue of superstars, banker Serge Semenenko and his wife, and photographer Alexis Waldeck.

Both of Thea's main shop assistants from London, Claudia Bruce and Boo Brassey (who was going out with Michael Butler at the time),[12] travelled over for the opening. Boo was photographed for *Women's Wear Daily*, modelling one of the dresses, while American *Vogue* also covered the launch, photographing three style icons (Warhol stars Jane Forth and 'Baby Jane' Holzer, as well as jewellery designer Elsa Peretti) lounging in the sumptuous environs of the new shop. Working as a model at the time, Peretti met Porter at a 'go-see' (a modelling audition) and appeared in two shows for her in New York. Generous as always, Thea gave her a green printed dress that she

Left A model wearing a
printed silk dress with
brocade panels at the press
lunch for the New York
opening. July 1971.

Below At the press view
in July 1971 inside the New
York shop a model wears
a chiffon jumpsuit made
from the same Sheila
Hudson fabric with polo
players as seen opposite.

Left Elsa Peretti modelling
a harlequin print silk dress
at the opening of the New
York shop, July 1971.

Below Two prints based on Persian paintings, designed by Sheila Hudson, are combined on the dress. One on the bodice with polo players, while on the sleeves and skirt is a single horseman with Persian style calligraphy at the hem of the skirt. Cherie Federau collection.

continued to wear for years afterwards. The shop's opening appeared to be an instant success: the day after the opening the 'serious fashion-mad flocked in'[13] with the Duchess of Windsor alone buying three pieces.

Described in the American press as 'totally liberated',[14] Thea's intellectual and seductive approach to fashion was novel to an industry that was more heavily structured around mass-market casualwear. She would fly back and forth from London every month or so, usually bringing the merchandise in her suitcases as it was almost all still produced in England. Being backed by a millionaire also had its perks: Butler would send a limousine to pick Porter up when she arrived in New York, which would then 'whisk [her] from Elaine's restaurant, to El Morocco and then back to Michael's apartment where Peter Yarrow would strum his guitar and sing until dawn for the enjoyment of guests such as Helmut Berger.'[15]

As the main couturier for notable men such as Butler and Yarrow, Porter was asked to create a special design in 1971 for Playboy's International Designer Collection, which was founded that year to 'encourage and recognize design excellence and innovation in men's fashion.'[16] With ensembles created by 60 leading designers – including Hardy Amies (1909–2003), Yves Saint Laurent and Pierre Cardin (b.1922) – the collection was exhibited at a gala event at the Plaza Hotel in New York that December. Thea's choice was a three-piece purple velvet evening suit (*opposite*).[17]

Although Thea was described as 'the designer of exotic clothes for beautiful people with beautiful incomes,'[18] Thea Porter New York closed after just six months. Porter was busy with the Greek Street shop in London, while Butler was involved in new theatre projects, leaving the staff he had hired with no real structure or support. A former production manager of *Hair* had been hired to run the shop but had no retail experience. Porter herself described the employees in New York as 'hippy amateurs' who scared away her best clients through their lack of attention.[19] The battle to maintain the high quality and consistency required for wholesale orders while operating such a small-scale establishment would plague Porter throughout her career, as would her general lack of understanding of business and how to adapt to mass-market production. The closure of the shop led to some difficulties in maintaining the burgeoning wholesale business in America, which would take several years to restore. Not easily daunted however, Thea would now shift her attention to the west coast of America to find new clients, and a new way of selling her clothes.

Opposite A three-piece velvet suit, with shirt made from Sandra Munro's patchwork print, designed for Playboy's inaugural menswear International Collection. Private collection.

Hollywood at-home

America was proving to be the ideal marketplace for Thea Porter clothes: a trip to Los Angeles in 1969 had helped to introduce Thea's work to a new group of clients – the wives of Hollywood actors and power brokers. Porter found California invigorating: 'The freedom, the light-stepping sense of well-being bred by the climate, the inordinate wealth of my customers and the lavishness of their lives, all these were addictive.'[1] Yet she realized how odd her situation was: 'Operating out of a small shop in London's sleazy Soho, I was providing extravagant party wear, the gilt on the gingerbread, for a rich and hedonistic society which partied every night.'[2] In 1970 Porter sold to private customers out of the Algonquin Hotel in New York; she also visited her client Neiman-Marcus in Dallas and attended to her Los Angeles buyers in Giorgio Beverly Hills and I. Magnin. Marylou Luther, the fashion editor of the *Los Angeles Times*, latched onto Porter's exotic designs as the apotheosis of a new type of at-home Hollywood dressing and the two became fast friends, with Thea's designs reappearing continually in Luther's column throughout the decade and Thea often staying with Luther and her husband on her visits to Los Angeles.

Trunk shows

Thea's designs found favour with the upper-class women of many American cities, particularly in the industrial capitals of Dallas and Detroit. In Detroit, *the* store to sell to was Hattie's in Bloomington Hills: it carried Jean Muir and Zandra Rhodes, and added Porter to its roster in 1972. According to Hattie's

Hollywood celebrity   Laura McLaws Helms

co-founder Linda Dresner, there was a group of women in Michigan who were interested in fashion, in shape, had money and loved to look pretty – for them the 'fantasy' aspect of Thea Porter dresses was very appealing.[3] In May 1974 a catwalk show of Thea's collection was put on at the Troy Hilton, in a suburb of Detroit, where 'models were transformed into a series of fairy-tale princesses,'[4] while Hattie's gave a trunk show for Porter, introducing her to all of their customers. From then on, Porter's clothes would be sent to Hattie's (and later to Linda Dresner's eponymous shop) for a bi-annual trunk show, from which all of the customers would place their orders (only a few pieces were ordered as stock due to their high retail price). This trunk sale method worked very successfully, and was replicated in numerous other shops.

Left Produced by Bianchini-Férier, this spangled fabric was heavily used by Porter in the mid-1970s. According to Porter 'the spangles dropped off in showers' and it was impossible to dry clean but her customers loved it. *Los Angeles Times Home Magazine*, 26 January 1975. Photograph by David Alexander.

Stars and celebrities

Those who primarily frequented Thea's Los Angeles trunk shows were the wives of famous Hollywood stars: Veronique Peck (wife of Gregory), Shirlee Fonda (wife of Henry), Joanna Carson (wife of Johnny), Felicia Lemmon (wife of Jack) and Carol Matthau (wife of Walter), among many others. These women would buy Thea's designs in multiples: one dress in ten different colours; a blouse in four; a jacket in five different fabrics. The Chazara jacket (see p.54), which Porter launched in 1975, became an instant hit, beloved for its flattering cut and intriguing mix of textures and patterns (Porter reported in her memoir that Shirlee Fonda collected over 60 of them).[5] Easily recognizable, the media took notice of her devotees and Porter's name became closely linked with an idea of high-class Hollywood dressing. One of the most important gossip columnists in Hollywood, Joyce Haber, used Porter's designs in her exposé novel, *The Users* (1976), as shorthand to describe this world and their customs: 'Tonight she looked wispy and feminine in the full-length Thea Porter chiffon that she and Natalie had selected at Giorgio's.'[6]

The most extravagant request came from Barbra Streisand, who ordered dresses to match each room of her Los Angeles home. Describing the order in 1975, Thea said: 'She kept saying that the colours in the sitting room were orange and grey and that she had a steel fireplace, which came from a 1928 building so she had to have a dress that went absolutely with that room, and she had to have another dress that went with an Art Nouveau kind of room – so I wondered what she was going to do in the corridor – if she was going to change rapidly in the corridor as she went from room to room!'[7] Streisand wore the resulting grey *abaya* on the cover of *House Beautiful* in August 1974; she also chose several of her own Porter designs to dress her character in the remake of *A Star is Born* (1976), including an evening gown of embellished Indian chiffon and a liquid silver lace sheath with matching shawl.

With designs such as these, Thea was creating custom-made garments that exuded a timeless quality, which ultimately kept her clients returning. Throughout her career, although most of Porter's designs were unique, the garments were, however, '*prêt-à-porter-de-luxe*' rather than French-style couture.[8] While Porter rarely made the same dress in the same fabrics and trims more than once, her designs did not require the same exactitude of tailoring as that of a Dior suit or Givenchy gown, and though she kept on hand the measurements of her best clients, these were used as a guide rather than strict instructions.

One of her favourite clients was Veronique Peck (see *overleaf*), who also dressed in Yves Saint Laurent, Givenchy and Guy Laroche couture. According to Veronique, 'Thea was a kind of ... in between ... boutique and couture',[9] as her clothes were individual yet did not require multiple fittings. For a special occasion, Mrs Peck would often call the shop in London from Los Angeles

This white chiffon dress with Indian-style gold sequin embroidery was worn by Veronique Peck to the 1979 Academy Awards. Cecilia Peck collection. Photograph by Amanda Charchian.

Above Elizabeth Taylor wearing a black chiffon open-fronted *abaya* with red and blue metallic embroidery in the Algonquin Hotel, Thea's base in New York. Taylor would purchase several *abayas* from Porter at every trunk show. *New York Post*, 12 August 1977. Photograph by Hernandez. V&A: AAD/1995/4/22

Above right Elizabeth Taylor wearing an *abaya* in a scene from *Zee and Co.* (1972). Filmed in the Greek Street shop.

to explain an event, and Porter would make something specifically for that. There was no discussion of how it would look and rarely were sketches sent: the finished outfit would arrive, sight unseen, and as Veronique disclosed, 'it would always be right ... she just really knew and understood, she was very sensitive and artistic and creative.'[10] An occasional alteration was required by her seamstress in Los Angeles to perfect the fit, but even Porter's more tailored garments had a certain looseness of cut that allowed for less precision than traditional haute couture. For clients like Veronique Peck, who spent many hours being fitted in the salons of Paris, this approach was novel and useful, especially when they needed a spectacular, one-of-a-kind garment very quickly. As Thea explained: 'I am fussy, though people think I am not. I am a perfectionist and try desperately hard to achieve perfection, or what I imagine it to be. If customers want to go through with all the boredom of coming back several times for fittings, everything has to be perfect: it is not that the rich have more time, it is just that they want value for money.'[11]

On screen

Other Hollywood clients brought Thea in to design not only their personal wardrobes, but also their on-set regalia. Although Edith Head had designed and produced Elizabeth Taylor's costumes for her role as the Queen of Light in George Cukor's *The Bluebird* (1976), Taylor insisted that they be made by Thea, who closed the Greek Street shop for a week of private fittings in mid-1975 in order to do so:

No woman has given me greater pleasure to dress. I cannot claim that Elizabeth Taylor has a model girl's figure: she is small and plump. Her body swells and retreats according to mood and diet. She has no illusions about herself: "I have to wear all these diamond rings", she would say apologetically, "because my fingers are so short". Yet she has a radiance and a natural physical dignity unmatched in my experience. She shares with Princess Margaret an uncanny quality: the whites of her eyes reflect colour. She used to call me her "magic lady".[12]

Of *The Bluebird*, Thea wrote: 'Among the costumes I made for her were a rich hoard of *kaftans*, light as air – some mauve and spangled, others shimmering silver, some in sleek satin, and always three of each.'[13] These diaphanous, sparkling garments were as well-suited for the movie screen as they were for a life of luxuriant hedonism. Outlandish designs such as these, created purely for spectacle, had much in common with Porter's non-theatrical designs in their use of all-over embellishment and diaphanous fabrics – pointing to an increasingly direct connection between fashion and costume. Previously Taylor had worn several more subdued Thea Porter pieces in *Zee and Co* (1972), the film adaptation of the novel by one of Porter's best friends, Edna O'Brien and which was partly shot in Greek Street, 'bringing business to a standstill'.[14] These opportunities arose due to the actor often wearing Porter's designs in her private life; she bought six garments in one go at a 1978 Thea Porter trunk show in New York.

With the help of her high-profile clients and press agents, Thea and her designs continued to be featured in the American media; interviews recounted the purchasing habits of her famous customers, many of whom Porter found difficult to sympathize with. To *Newsweek* in 1977, she explained: *I think I'd rather not be friends just with my customers because I have to get away from what I do all day. I suppose inside I'm still very puritan about this whole thing of being extravagant about clothes and only thinking about clothes. And while I feel that my entire life is in search of beauty, and I want to make women look beautiful and I adore beautiful fabrics, beautiful fabrics are frightfully expensive. So there's a guilt feeling as well.*[15]

Giorgio Beverly Hills

Although New York had proved to be a difficult market partly due to the managerial inadequacy of the set-up, sales in Los Angeles continued to increase steadily, mainly thanks to Thea's connection with experienced retail merchandisers such as Giorgio Beverly Hills. The most exclusive shop in Los Angeles, Giorgio's had a bar, a café and was organized in a manner that allowed the clients to 'hang around for three or four hours',[16] trying clothes on and often leaving with up to 20 pieces. Fred Hayman, the owner of Giorgio's, and his wife, Gayle, had first encountered Porter's designs on a buying trip to London at the beginning of the decade; by 1973 Porter had expanded into the

Right Britt Ekland in a
brocaded silk *abaya* in
the Los Angeles home she
shared with Rod Stewart
in 1975. She wore the same
abaya for an advertisement
for Sanderson wallpapers
in 1973. Photograph
by David Steen.

sales of exclusive custom-made ready-to-wear pieces for Giorgio's – usually
producing a single-size run of each garment ordered, with each featuring
a slightly different trim. By the middle of the decade, Giorgio was Porter's
largest wholesale account, valued at $300,000 a year. Fred Hayman recalls:
'We did very well with her line. It was a unique line ... we sold it enormously
well ... [The women who bought the clothes] were adventuresome because
they were different than any other clothes.'[17] According to actress Lorna Luft
(the daughter of Hollywood legend Judy Garland): 'You loved when somebody
said, "Thea Porter's got new things in the store." You just ran – you didn't
even stop and you never collected $200, you just ran. It was like Monopoly –
go right directly to the store.'[18]

Thea remembered there being 'an insatiable demand' for the Gipsy dresses,
while the *abayas* were also much requested by Giorgio's customers; Britt
Ekland purchased them to wear around the Hollywood home she shared with
singer Rod Stewart (*above*). Having extended her design repertoire beyond the
more close evocations of non-Western dress to include a more fully rounded
wardrobe, it was sometimes difficult for Porter to agree to produce the
requested quantity of her signature designs – she was always 'eager to move
on to other designs irrespective of what the market wanted.'[19]

Though she had had difficulty in fulfilling wholesale orders for years, it was only in 1978 that Giorgio's finally (and rather acrimoniously) severed ties with the designer, due to the late arrival of orders that were often incomplete. Having been the largest account, this termination reduced Thea's income dramatically. At the same time, with her associates, she continued to seek possible investment and licensing opportunities, even approaching her client Veronique Peck to produce a joint line of '"night cosmetics", a scent, dolls, household linens … and décor, clothes, hose, etc. etc.'[20] Again this opportunity progressed little beyond a series of informal letters: Thea never had the wherewithal to exploit her high-powered clients for business gains. She often spoke rather candidly and indiscreetly to the press about her clients' bodies and purchases. In a 1978 interview she said of Elizabeth Taylor, 'She creamed off the four best kaftans in the collection. But they look divine on her. It doesn't matter how fat she is,' while Princess Margaret was described as, 'Very imperious'.[21]

Other clients fared rather better in her estimations: actress Bianca Jagger ('She outchics anyone. She can wear anything, do anything and still be amazingly elegant.'[22]) and Lauren Bacall ('Everything looks right on her. It's that length of leg.'[23]). Having discovered Thea's designs while shopping at Giorgio Beverly Hills one day, the country singer Crystal Gayle visited the Greek Street shop and commissioned Porter to design several costume changes for her 1979 CBS TV special (*opposite*).[24] Porter studied the singer's facial expressions and body movements, seeing her as a '… romantic, even though she has a country-western image. I made her look like a bird of paradise.'[25] The strapless knee-length cocktail dresses were modified from the Spring 1979 collection to highlight Crystal's famous hip-length hair. Gayle recalls: 'You know how people click with certain designers? She was petite [like me] … so I think that's where we probably had some of the same ideas and she was just putting her special touches on the clothes … Looking back, I trusted her as I really liked what she was doing with all of her designs.'[26] Porter added more embellishment and shortened several of the designs, providing greater sparkle and drama for the camera; the broadcast and subsequent publicity furthered her direct influence over street fashion, high fashion and popular culture at large.

'Hard work and hard partying'

At this time, Thea was still travelling to New York twice a year and Los Angeles once a year, and after the Paris shop opened in 1977, she would also commute across the Channel weekly. With a fluid and open social life, and friendships with important people, these trips were awash with hard work and hard partying. Porter's former shop assistant Jonty Scott recalls how 'Thea would quite happily sit with Andy Warhol and smoke a joint, and then go to 54.'[27] Her assistant at the time, Fiona Dunlop, remembers Porter running up astronomical bills at the Algonquin on a trip in 1977, which they

were only able to pay after their last sale. She recalls that the final client was 'haggling away like crazy and in the end I just did a deal because I knew we had to sell these last dresses in order to pay the bill. It was a very Thea kind of thing.'[28] By 1978, in an interview for *People* magazine in her hotel suite showroom, surrounded by socialites fighting over $3,000 *abayas*, Porter admitted to feeling drained 'and terribly tired'. Through all of these highs, the strain of opening the Paris shop had taken its toll on Porter, and on her company as a whole: the hard slog required to maintain the momentum of an international business, satisfying the American market, and the intensive life/work balance that Porter endured as a result, became apparent only as her health deteriorated and her company faltered.

France had been important to Thea Porter from the very start of her career in interior decoration. She accumulated textiles from everywhere, but notably from Lyons – for centuries the centre of the French silk industry.[1] A frequent visitor to the city, Porter often purchased fabrics there, and then used many of the same fabrics as the *haute couturiers* in Paris, such as Bianchini-Férier's satins and silks, and Staron's *moiré de laine*.[2] Others remember Porter travelling to Paris for the day simply to pick up yards of antique gold lamé and other pieces to be used in her designs (p.126).[3]

A Parisian outpost

Business expansion in 1971 was projected for Thea by one of her many astrologers. At the beginning of the year she travelled to Paris and New York to look into setting up shops there, and, in Paris, took a space on the rue Dauphine. Cards were printed announcing her Parisian outpost but it became ensnarled in a mess of legal matters and leases; she would have to wait until 1977 to open a shop there.[4] In 1974 Porter rented a small flat in Paris at 66 rue des Saints Pères in Saint-Germain. With exposed beams and an attic-like feel, it was decorated in much the same manner as her home and shop in London: Iraqi carpets covered the tile floors while the windows were draped with hand-painted chiffons by Hannah Meckler (see p.84).

In November 1975 Princess Sabine Poniatowski, who ran a glamorous boutique out of her Parisian flat, organized a show of Porter's collection at the Art Deco-inspired restaurant Maxim's, which was well attended by all of Parisian high society. The Thea Porter line began to gain attention in Paris

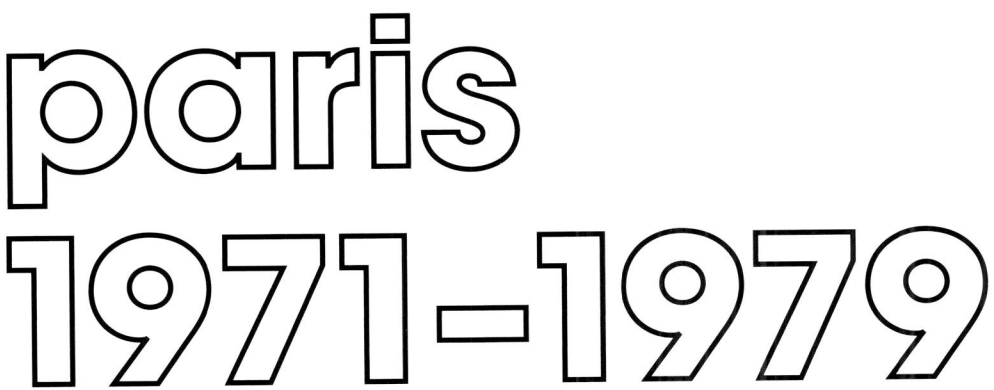

paris
1971-1979

The home of haute couture

Laura McLaws Helms

and fulfil a personal ambition for Porter herself: 'an early show at Maxim's in Paris whetted my appetite for a more permanent presence there. I have always had an insane longing for Paris.'[5] Porter's French-Tunisian mother combined with her upbringing in Francophone Syria meant that she not only spoke fluent French but had a deep love of French art and literature (she would carry a copy of the first volume of Marcel Proust's *A la recherche du temps perdu* in her bag until she died).[6] Although she had never previously lived in Paris, she felt deeply linked to the city. After the success of the show at Maxim's, she moved to a grander flat: '... all mirrored doors, springy parquet floors, and sublime views across the Luxemburg [*sic*] gardens',[7] where she would present her collection to buyers and private clients. This led to a deal with a manufacturer in Paris to produce a line of high-end, ready-to-wear garments, labelled 'théa porter france'. Launched in April 1976, the 25-piece collection included chic, black lace separates elegantly trimmed with antique gold braid.

Throughout these years, there was always romance in her life. Thea formally divorced Bob in 1967, but she had begun to stray while they were still married in Lebanon (in a 1973 interview she recounts an affair with a Spanish diplomat whom she would meet secretly to discuss art).[8] Though shy and quite unassuming, Porter enjoyed frequenting parties and wanted a partner with her. Her longest relationship was with a French-Lebanese TV producer, Antoine Giraco. They met in Beirut in the early 1960s, where he fell in love with her, and they would later reconnect in London in 1973. For much of the latter half of the 1970s they were a couple.

Théa Porter Paris, 1977–1979
With a boyfriend, a flat and a ready-to-wear line in Paris, the next step was a shop in the city. At this time Thea was connected by her banker friend Michael Meakin to a wealthy Saudi, Mohammed Kamel, interested in opening a *haute couture* salon. With his backing (and the advice of her 'French

Above This black, gold and silver *lamé* was based on a French fabric from 1810. It was probably sourced in Paris, and taken to London to cover the walls of the living room in Porter's flat, and as patches of some of the *abayas*.

soothsayers'), Théa Porter Paris opened on the rue de Tournon (*below*), on the Left Bank:

I opened the shop on April 1, 1977 with a hilarious launch attended by all the duchesses, princesses and belles élégantes of my acquaintance ... My own April Fool's joke that evening was to dress a six-foot-tall black American transvestite, who went by the name of Andrea in a white wedding dress which he showed off to great effect. Andrea ... most nights did a striptease act at L'Etrier.[9]

Prior to the opening, the Thea Porter Paris Winter 1977–8 collection was shown at the Paris shop in March 1977, in collaboration with British fashion designer Katharine Hamnett (p.80). Launching the collection and shop with support from her jet-set clientele, Porter looked to this venture as a means of securing her success in the industry and increasing the financial stability of the company. With her new base she now had access to highly skilled French seamstresses, and employed five to six workers in the basement atelier below the shop, which was run by well-seasoned Parisian *vendeuses*. Although she was largely unknown in France and had trouble getting press coverage, the Paris shop was much more modern in style than Thea's

Below Advertisement announcing the Paris shop, photographed in Porter's Bolton Street flat. *L'Officiel*, 1976. Photographs by Van Pariser.

Thea Porter
9 RUE DE TOURNON 75006 PARIS TEL 325 6986
8 GREEK STREET LONDON W 1 TEL. 437.07.81

Thea Porter
9 RUE DE TOURNON 75006 PARIS TEL 325 6986
8 GREEK STREET LONDON W 1 TEL. 437.07.81

Left Ensemble in black lace produced under the 'théa porter france' label in 1976. Exploiting Porter's trademark antique braids and subtly revealing cuts, the garments were often designed in a more classical style. Laura McLaws Helms collection. Photograph by Amanda Charchian.

Opposite Silk georgette gown with a thickly quilted patchwork bodice, first shown in white at Porter's 1975 event at Maxim's. This black version was worn by Veronique Peck for entertaining at her Beverly Hills home. Cecilia Peck collection. Photograph by Amanda Charchian.

'When I started the shop in Paris, I'd no idea it would be such hard work; it's not designing that is the problem, but the administration, and people to look after...'

Greek Street headquarters and was an attempt to break into the French fashion establishment. Beyond the difficulties of gaining recognition in a new market, the Paris outpost proved important in retaining Porter's cultural currency with American clients, who were impressed by her foray into the French fashion industry and saw it as a sign of cachet.

Porter's expensive representations of non-Western garments gained relevance thanks in part to the re-emergence of 'ethnic' fashion in the latter half of the decade (as seen predominantly in the work of designers Yves Saint Laurent and Kenzo Takada)[10] and a major exhibition of Russian peasant costume in 1976 at the Costume Institute at the Metropolitan Museum of Art in New York (curated by Thea's friend, former American *Vogue* editor Diana Vreeland, see *opposite*). As her clientele evolved from rich trust-fund hippies and youthful starlets to the wives of important actors and diplomats, so her clothes changed to suit their needs. Keeping the textiles and mystery that made the garments so unmistakably 'Thea Porter', they also needed to fulfil certain criteria: 'Many of my Paris customers wear my clothes to the Elysée Palace. They always say they can't be too dramatic, that they want to look pretty and fetching, but not outrageous.'[11] That year Princess Firyal of Jordan, a sister-in-law of King Hussein, ordered a dozen $700 patchwork dresses to give to her ladies-in-waiting. For Porter, this was a continuation of the social and aesthetic changes wrought by the hippie era, commenting at the time: 'Patchwork epitomizes the peasant lifestyle ... It's all part of an international desire to identify with the masses – even if you happen to live in a sumptuous palace.'[12]

Designing for the elite meant that Thea's garments had to be of the finest quality; so too did the atmosphere of the shop, as well as the champagne and client entertainment. The subsequent expenses were an effective form of advertising, helping Porter's designs remain the couture of choice for some of the best-dressed women in the world. Yet the heavy cost of setting up the shop in Paris meant that the company was in debt almost immediately.

Although not atypical for a new venture to start in debt, slow sales and a lack of financial structure behind Théa Porter Paris, prevented the new shop from repaying its investment. Even as early as 1968 in London these business issues were known, and yet never solved; a proposal for the introduction of additional capital, in 1968, states: 'With the burden of fittings, ordering and actual selling, it has not really been possible even to comply with the minimum system of keeping records of sales and cash expenditure.'[13]

Paris: A financial black hole

Following the opening in Paris, Porter would travel between London and Paris once or twice a week for the next two years. Chaotically disorganized, the whole business was, according to her daughter, 'basically suitcases full of clothes – she would just take them with her on the plane, made in London, sold there. Sometimes being made there and being brought back here, same with the States – just suitcases full of clothes going backward and forward in an incredibly haphazard way.'[14] Fiona Dunlop, an employee from Greek Street who moved to Paris to manage the shop there in late 1977, recalled that few purchases were made. Inevitably, Théa Porter Paris became a 'financial black hole',[15] and although the London shop continued to make sales, there was no way of monitoring the flow of money in or out of the company. Proceeds made from the sale of a garment would immediately be used to pay bills,

Below Letter from Diana Vreeland to Thea Porter, 11 June 1977. The two remained friends after Vreeland left American *Vogue*, and this letter to Porter thanks her for the gift of a jacket and shirt. Vreeland gives her impression of Olimpia de Rothschild after she saw her wearing a silver Porter ensemble. V&A: AAD/1995/4/11

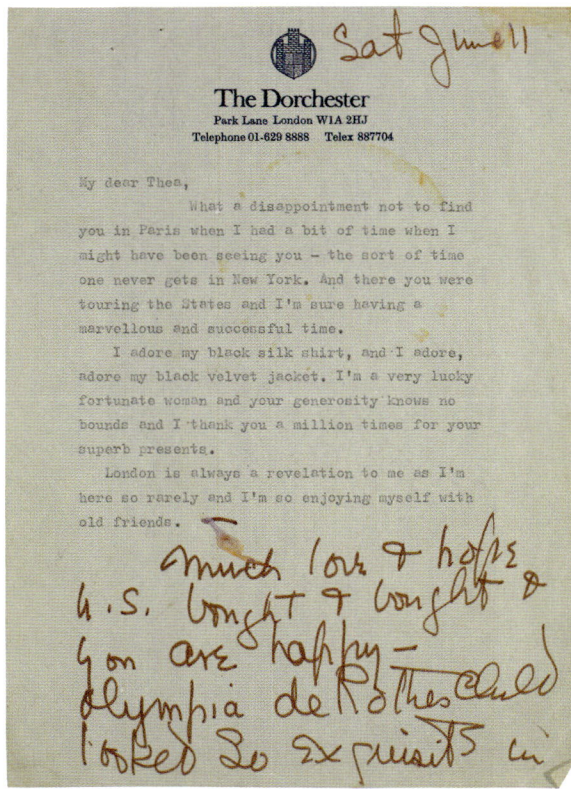

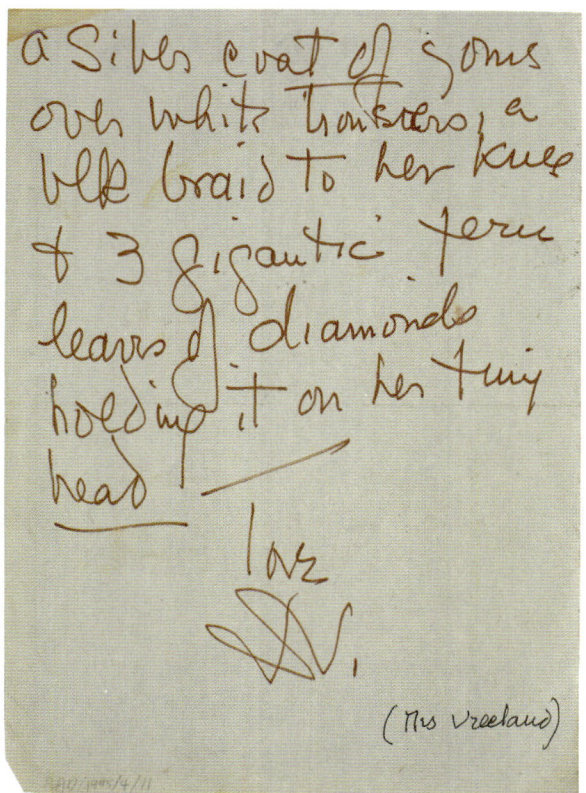

yet no record was made of these transactions, resulting in a total lack of understanding of the financial health of the business:

When I started the shop in Paris, I'd no idea it would be such hard work; it's not designing that is the problem, but the administration, and people to look after ... I've practically given up my social life now, I don't dare ring up my friends, I'm too tired for dinner-parties ... At least it's made me lose weight.[16]

Dunlop remembers Thea as 'a dreamer and law unto herself for whom money was no object – viz Paris apartment, her boyfriend Antoine, Swiss clinics, generous lunches at the Algonquin (for clients who were undoubtedly 100 times wealthier than her) & elsewhere. That was also her charm – her cultural breadth plus a kind of childlike naivety – but this same trait sometimes also impacted badly on a lot of people.'[17] When there was money in the bank Porter would often jet off to Switzerland for beauty treatments instead of paying her bills.

According to Thea's memoir, in the two years she travelled back and forth between London and Paris, £50,000 in cash disappeared from each location.[18] Since cash was often her preferred method of bill payment, it seems likely that this missing money was spent on fabric and bills, as well as supporting Porter's personal lifestyle. Porter's former assistant, Louise Fennell remembered that: 'It was always a struggle. Everything was a struggle ... She was fantastically generous and free with the way she spent money. So if she had any, it just went very quickly. It was awful. Paris particularly was very bad. I think there was a lot of partying and a lot of taking masses of clients and potential clients out, just frittering it away.'[19]

Challenges and disasters

Other than the inclusion of some garments in the occasional editorial, however, Porter made little headway with the French fashion press. Her most glamorous pieces would appear in the party pages of French *Vogue*, as worn by socialites such as Olimpia de Rothschild and Princess Caracciolo. Likewise, the champagne breakfast and fashion presentation Porter hosted in 1978 at her Paris apartment was attended by the *crème de la crème* of the aristocracy, with her address book containing long lists of countesses and princesses. But the fashion industry in Paris ran differently to that of her home ground in London:

To my chagrin, however, I discovered that the grand French do not very often buy grand clothes: they prefer to borrow them for an evening and return them, neatly pressed of course, the next day. The idea is that they are doing you a favour in being seen in your clothes. If one of my salesgirls so much as hesitated to lend a dress, the customer would snap, "all right then, I have a cousin who works at Givenchy and I will borrow a dress from her. But I must say yours are more fun!" Such compliments buttered no parsnips.[20]

Opposite An elaborately embellished dress made from black sari fabric, with matching veil, from Thea Porter's Autumn/Winter 1979 collection. Photograph by David Seidner.

At the same time as the shop's finances were deteriorating, so too was Porter's relationship with Antoine Giraco. Leaving Paris for an extended stay in London, Thea returned to her Paris flat near the Luxembourg gardens to find that everything of value had been taken: according to her records, £100,000 worth of antiques, which she said he sold to dealers around the city.[21] Shaken by the brutality of the theft and the incompetency of the police in helping her, Porter was left impoverished. The French detectives shied away from involvement due to Giraco's plea that he was owed money due to his unpaid management of the Paris shop.[22] The two never spoke again, although mutual friends recall him still speaking lovingly of Porter long after this time.

Thea's Parisian endeavour began with much excitement, but the final months of the business on both sides of the Channel were shrouded in chaos. According to her business notes, in 1979 an offer was made by a South African businessman to raise £100,000 for her enterprise (ironically, from Kamel who had invested in the Paris shop).[23] Although discussions took place, the designer decided against accepting and the money was then invested in fellow London-based designer Ossie Clark. Without the necessary capital, the shop closed in 1979; Thea continued to visit Paris but did not show there again. Yet despite the tumultuous and chaotic business and personal atmosphere, Porter's designs from this period remained remarkably on point – the Autumn/Winter 1979–80 collection was composed of fanciful cocktail dresses with heavily beaded bodices and flowing chiffon skirts (p.133), as well as high-necked evening gowns made of expensive guipure lace, mirroring similar styles in the *haute couture* collections of Yves Saint Laurent, Christian Dior and Nina Ricci that season.

Earlier that year business broker Robert Chenciner had introduced Thea to Peter Salmon who proposed a venture to market Thea Porter products worldwide, negotiations for which went to the contract and trademark stage.[24] These businessmen had 'strategic and marketing skills and experience' and sought to 'co-operate together to maximize royalties from sales of products designed or approved by Mrs Porter.'[25] According to Porter, she withdrew from these negotiations following notification by her lawyer that Chenciner and Salmon were interested in reselling the company quickly for profit rather than working to develop it. This deal would have come at a time when investment was badly needed in Théa Porter Paris and Thea Porter Decorations Ltd, the latter of which might possibly have been saved by favourable financing and organized business managers.[26]

Years of collecting non-Western textiles and frequenting antique markets had sustained the continual evolution of Porter's creative eye as she encountered new inspiration on every trip. The incorporation of earlier silhouettes and details called for a high level of research, and Porter devoted herself completely: 'Endlessly going around the *Puces* and all those French

Above This kimono-style jacket was wrapped around the body and worn with a matching pink-sashed skirt. The caption to the photograph was 'On the line ... bound hips, slits, great coat'. British *Vogue*, December 1976. Photograph by Norman Parkinson.

markets, picking up bits of old costumes and dissecting them and using those shapes and then injecting her own brand of magic.'[27] Perhaps business in Paris had not been financially successful, and business opportunities had been missed, but the creative process, the immersion in yet another culture and the exposure to another glamorous, chic and well-connected clientele ultimately meant that Porter's designs remained appealing, covetable and timeless.

For all of the success that Thea Porter had achieved in her fashion career – the large orders, the magazine covers, the high-profile clients – a general lack of good business sense and the resulting financial instability cloaked much of it in a semi-constant anxiety. Even though the company was run in a decidedly unprofessional manner, Porter's *emporium de luxe* still featured in the media, and was noted in *Harpers & Queen*'s list of the best shops in London in 1977: 'Exotic materials, beaded and embroidered and spangled, and mixed together into ravishing evening dresses in Mrs Porter's Soho shop. Decidedly Eastern flavour much beloved by British women with a yearning for the *yashmak*.'[1] With the high cost of her garments ($975 for an off-the-rail printed silk chiffon tunic with matching belt and black chiffon skirt, in 1976),[2] it was difficult to sell enough garments to consistently make a profit.

Described by the *New York Times* in 1977 as 'one of London's legends',[3] Porter conducted discussions throughout the 1970s with various parties regarding possible ready-to-wear manufacturing and licensing deals in America, in order to bring in capital and security, yet none came to fruition, due in large part to poor business advice. Having encountered innumerable problems in regards to production within the United Kingdom, in 1978 she attempted to set up a ready-to-wear side of her business manufactured in India, where she found that the quality of production she required (particularly the embroidery) could be produced more cheaply than in Europe. A small collection of garments was manufactured but due to a lack of financial backing, she was unable to continue this endeavour.

london
1976–1989

Collaborations and new beginnings   *Laura McLaws Helms*

Worsening matters, as the wholesale business grew, her team lacked the business knowledge or the monetary resources to keep up with the expansion. Thea Porter Decorations Ltd was run out of one small shop, a 'cottage-industry' as Louise Fennell described it, for the majority of Porter's career with most work being done by outworkers in their own homes, which was more expensive than producing the whole collection in a single location.[4] In addition, the difficulty in regulating pattern grading and other production issues when working with a variety of out-workers meant that sometimes orders would be sent back by department stores due to inconsistencies. The profit margin with these clothes was low – which comes as little surprise as Porter still used the same expensive fabrics, meaning that less money was earned on them compared with the pieces purchased directly from her shop (*opposite*). In hindsight, it is apparent that it was not a lack of demand for Thea Porter's designs, but rather her workshop's inability to keep up with orders that eventually led to the loss of her main wholesale accounts – some more disruptive than others (as in the case of Giorgio Beverly Hills in 1978 – see p.120).

Experiments with ready-to-wear

Notwithstanding these setbacks, Thea made another attempt at ready-to-wear for Autumn/Winter 1980, with wholesale prices averaging from £50 to £100 per garment (as compared with around £200 to £600 for her main line). With a new logo, the ready-to-wear line included a silk satin quilted jacket that sold for £120, while the main collection was composed of crinkly gold *lamé* separates and large tulle ball gowns embroidered with lilies of the valley.

As Porter was unwilling to lower the quality of the textiles she used, this often meant that far more money was being spent than was being earned. To make matters worse, when the rent for the Greek Street shop trebled to £35,000 a year in the summer of 1980,[5] breaking even became impossible and the closure of the shop was announced in October of that year. There followed yet more bad news: a successful selling trip to America in 1981 ended in disaster when Porter returned to London to discover that her accountants had advised her bank to reduce her current overdraft from £26,000 to £6,000, leaving her unable to make up the orders she had just received.

Following the closure of the Soho shop at the end of January, the liquidation was announced in the press on 5 February 1981; the company had debts of £48,000.[6] Louise Fennell, who worked for Porter up until the end of Greek Street, recalled:

There were always bookkeepers trying desperately to make sense of the madness ... always playing catch up. There was never enough cash flow. Whenever anything was sold, it was always, "Let's order masses of fabrics from Bianchini-Férier, and we'll deal with the bill when it comes" ... In those days, you could order things, and they sent you the bill.

Right One-shoulder variation of the halterneck evening gown shown in the sketch below. Autumn/Winter 1980 collection. Lauren Lepire collection. Photograph by Amanda Charchian.

Above Sketch and fabric sample for a halterneck evening gown. Autumn/Winter 1980 collection. V&A: AAD/1995/4/23

Thea was really good at ordering a lot of stuff regardless of what it cost. So she always said, "My accountant's ripped me off." They didn't. It was just uncontrolled spending.[7]

It was not, however, solely Thea's unwieldy financial acrobatics that heralded the end of Greek Street: the world of fashion and society had changed over the years that she had been in business in Soho. Keith Goodman, the chartered accountant nominated as liquidator, remarked following the announcement: 'The world's elegant women are not prepared to go to a place surrounded by sex shops and strip clubs and populated by pimps and prostitutes.'[8] What was once seen as a fun excursion during a period when forays into rebellion and countercultural living were commonplace for high society, a more conservative mind-set (encouraged by recession and a change of government) had returned luxury shopping to the most expensive postcodes. Porter was not the only one of her contemporaries to encounter financial difficulties at this time: Ossie Clark went out of business the same week with debts of £200,000 while John Bates had entered voluntary liquidation a month earlier. Called 'the textile trade's worst recession since the war' by *The Times*, out of the 'Designs on Fashion' group from 1973 (see p.100–1) only Muir and Rhodes were seen to be surviving at full strength in 1981.[9] Five days after the liquidation was announced, Porter gave a lecture, 'Paintings – Fashion and Art', at the London Fashion Forum; not one to be bowed by failure, Thea bravely faced her business setbacks and maintained her vision.

Following the formation of a new company that same year (Thea Porter Ltd), the designer worked for the next few years out of a number of different locations but was never able to rival her earlier success, mainly due to a lack of capital. The negative publicity from the liquidation, compounded by the absence of a definite headquarters for her work made it difficult for many customers to keep up with her whereabouts. Having left Greek Street in 1981, for six months she traded out of her Bolton Street maisonette before moving into a small first floor space on Avery Row, near Bond Street – a more sedate location than Soho. A month after liquidation Porter had rallied enough to open London Fashion Week with a champagne brunch *defilé* at her then-boyfriend's restaurant, Langan's Brasserie, on 30 March.

Describing the 1980s as 'a descent from the dizzy peaks of the previous decade, an awakening to harsh realities,'[10] Porter continued to design and produce collections throughout the disorder: at the 1981 Langan's show she exhibited 'ruffled lace jackets to throw on over brocaded satin evening dresses, strapless printed cotton styles and moiré taffeta knickerbockers' (*opposite*);[11] and in January 1982, she travelled to Los Angeles and gave the last of many trunk shows at the home of Veronique and Gregory Peck. While there she gave an interview to the *Los Angeles Times*, intelligently pulling apart the new fashion tribes of London – the teenage 'baby-faced monsters',

Above **Sarah Tremlett wearing an embroidered gauze evening top and moiré skirt from Thea Porter's Autumn/Winter 1980 collection. Photograph by David Whyte.**

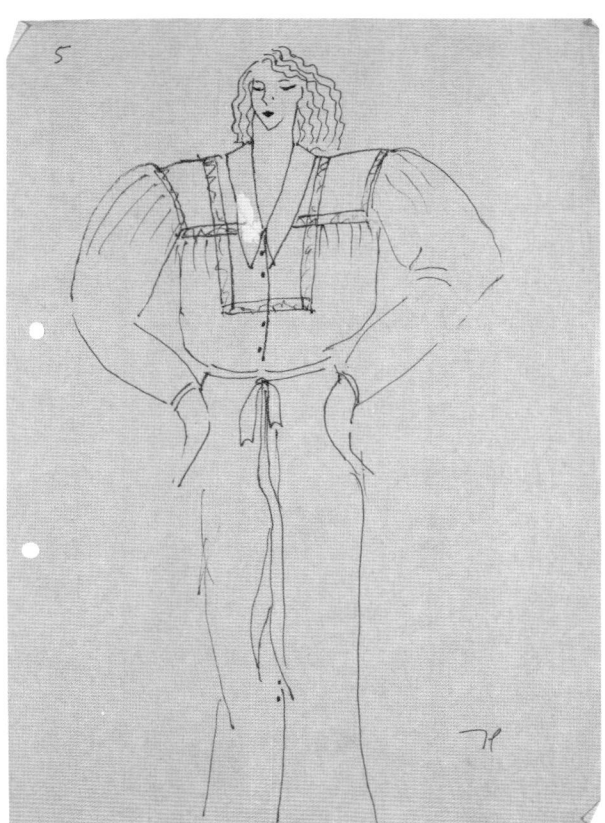

the 'Sloane Rangers', the 'punky-debbie creatures' and the 'black-belt shoppers' – none of whom were aligned with her own vision of beauty and culture.

In 1982, Thea Porter completed a commission for several outfits for a TV movie, *A Married Man*, produced by London Weekend Television (LWT) and worn by American actress Lise Hilboldt. But not all collaborations were as successful. Cognizant of the ups and downs of her business, Porter later wrote of her 'triumphs and disasters';[12] one of these disasters took place in early 1982 when the renowned theatre director Robert Wilson, of the Byrd Hoffman Foundation, visited Thea in Paris to discuss whether she could organize the costumes for his new project – *Great Day in the Morning* – a 'black opera' set in the nineteenth century starring Jessye Norman. Wilson originally wanted Porter to design some of the clothes and hire the rest, but due to a lack of period clothes available to rent in Paris, she was to make them all. Porter flew to Paris three times with her sketches and costumes, each time finding the cast and requirements to have changed. Late-arriving letters with complaints from Wilson, along with evolving production decisions, left Porter in the lurch professionally and financially: due to her faith in the project, she was out of pocket on all production costs. Wilson and Thea decided to part ways with none of her costumes being used in the final performances, but she was only repaid £1,417 of the £14,405 owed

Dresses with boleros
attached or with cape
attached

for materials and manufacture. Later she would feel disappointed that her
involvement with the project felt incomplete.[13]

Despite moving to Beauchamp Place at the end of 1982, the shop was on
a top floor, invisible from the street, and Porter found it difficult to gain new
customers or reconnect with her established clientele. Nevertheless, a core
group of women she had been dressing for over a decade continued to order
in bulk (up to ten items at a time), and Porter, as indefatigable as ever, was
able to continue creating in the face of financial adversity; her collection
for Spring/Summer 1984 was again shown at Langan's and included an
array of tunics with hand-appliquéd tiger stripes, puff-sleeved floral
dresses and slinky silk jumpsuits (*opposite*).

Throughout the decade, further attempts to expand her business came
to nothing. In 1986 Porter briefly worked with Princess Dina of Jordan
who owned a shop called Arabesque on Motcomb Street (the idea was that
Porter's clothes would be sold alongside 'Arabian style' *kaftans* made by
other designers), but the two women parted company after a few months
(p.145). By this time her health was gradually fading, with erratic behaviour
and the beginnings of memory loss characteristic of the Alzheimer's that
would later lay claim to her faculties: 'When she started going downhill,
lots of people just weren't interested. She was losing her client base. There
were a few people who continued to be loyal … but she wasn't producing as
much stuff …'[14]

Above Sketches of dresses
with boleros or capes in
one of Thea's sketchbooks.
The defined shoulders
and triangular silhouettes
are in keeping with trends
of the 1980s.
V&A: AAD/1995/4/16

Opposite Thea Porter
showed her collections
at Langan's Brasserie in
Mayfair from 1981 to the
mid-1980s. Her Spring/
Summer 1984 collection
was a mix of easy-to-wear
dresses and suits,
alongside satin evening
tunics, hand-appliquéd
with tiger stripes.
Photographs by
Desmond O'Neill.

Thea Porter -185

Opposite A striped silk wrap-over dress from Porter's 1985 collection; it was at this time that she closed the shop on Beauchamp Place, and began working with Princess Dina at Arabesque.

Below Thea Porter and Princess Dina of Jordan during their brief partnership. Arabesque (Princess Dina's shop), Motcomb Street, London, 1986.

Thea Porter's Scrapbook: enduring friendships (1986–2000)

Thea at this point began to examine her life and career, and decided to write a memoir, which she called 'Thea Porter's Scrapbook'. She took pleasure in reconnecting with people from her past; recognizing her faltering memory, she took notes and recorded interviews with friends, clients and people who had worked for her. The fully illustrated book was to consist of three main sections: 'The Lure of the Exotic', 'The story of Greek street', and 'What are clothes about'. This last chapter ended with the inventory of the wardrobe of a Venetian notable, Giorgio Ruzzini, who died on a ship travelling from Venice to Alexandria in 1453. As Thea described it: 'the inventory of his wardrobe found in his ironbound chest may serve to illustrate the utilitarian as well as the life-enhancing functions – the sheer panache – of his clothes'; a theme she had always wanted to extend to her own designs.[15]

A visible example of the deep loyalty and love she engendered in others can be gleaned from a former boyfriend from the early 1970s, Tony Johnson, who stepped in to help take care of her living expenses after the closure of

Opposite In 1981
the Central Office of
Information in London
made a film about Porter.
Lebanese writer Hanan
al-Shaykh modelled the
clothes in the Orientalist
setting of Leighton House.

her business.[16] The death of her former lover Peter Langan in 1988 brought tragedy and deep despair into her life – the anguish of being unable to prevent his suicide was a trauma that catapulted her into a place of unreality. Yet through it all, Thea Porter continued to design clothes for close friends and family into the early 1990s, and as late as 1991 she asked Janet Taylor to print a new 'Tulip' silk for her. But after several years of increasingly confused thinking and behaviour, the designer was finally diagnosed with Alzheimer's in 1994.[17]

Throughout her years in London, Porter had become known for her personal generosity. Those who knew Porter spoke fondly of her: 'Thea is not rich, however opulent her designs. She gives away her money and her dresses with a generosity as dramatic as it is foolish.'[18] Her friend B Larsson recalled how Thea gave her an orange *abaya* to match the walls of her newly painted sitting room, and she always ensured that her marine archaeologist friend Honor Frost had something suitable to wear to one of her many lectures.[19] The author Hanan al-Shaykh, whom Porter had persuaded to model for her at a photo shoot at Leighton House in the late 1981 (*opposite*) recalled how, upon refusing to accept a dress as a gift, Thea sent her several boxes of the most expensive orchids instead. Other friends remember her floating into parties, trailing chiffon, and bringing champagne and bouquets of lilies along too. Andrew Logan remembered: 'She was very refined; she was a very beautiful creature, quite small but very delicate ... but with a rod of iron.'[20] This strength of character and determination to keep going whatever crisis she encountered, personal or financial, ensured her work would continue to be relevant: 'Single-handedly, she has managed ... to make herself a major fashion force, not only here [London] but in New York and on the Continent. Her clothes are Britain's best couture.'[21]

Afterword

'*Tout casse, tout passe, tout lasse*' are the words Thea's family chose for her gravestone.[1] It was a proverb she repeated often, and which evoked a life lived for the moment, her wonderful sense of fun and a fierce independence of spirit, combined with a deep sense of fatalism and stoicism in the face of adversity.

Religion had played an important role in Thea's early life – the Bible her parents gave her in 1937, when she was ten years old, bore the inscription: This book will keep you from Sin or Sin will keep you from this Book', and her relationship with the faith of her Presbyterian parents was to remain a complex one throughout her life. Thea and her brother Patrick acquired a strong work ethic from their parents, as well as an extraordinary kindness and generosity: attributes that are remembered by all who knew her.[2]

Thea's memoir, or 'scrapbook' (as she referred to it), has served as an important basis for this publication: written before her illness, it gives a strong sense of what inspired and drove her, and what she considered important in shaping her career. 'I spent all my waking hours, and indeed much of the night (barring the parties), wrestling with clothes, dreaming them up in my mind's eye, struggling to capture the fleeting image on paper, translating it into fabric and hanging it on to a woman's body so as to make that body more alluring, more beautiful.'[3] For Thea, the beauty she strived to achieve for her customers was a delicate balance between creating garments that were put together like paintings, that made the wearer feel beautiful, that could effortlessly combine a wealth of fabrics (from Damascus brocades, to saris or specially commissioned prints) and yet did not detract from 'the primacy of the face'.[4] She would remind us that: 'in the end a dress is just a dress';[5] it was this approach to fashion design that made her garments distinctive and endowed them with an enduring and continuing appeal. As a journalist once commented: 'never in, never out'.[6]

In drawing together the threads that make up the sophisticated vision and aesthetic that led to Thea's extraordinary achievement, it was her Syrian-Francophone childhood that was key. For here was her first encounter with what has so mesmerized those who have ever visited Damascus, or Aleppo; until so recently, the ancient bustling *suq*s filled with traditional luscious fabrics, carpets, inlaid mother-of-pearl furniture, or opaline glass; the legacy of the great artistic traditions of the Ottomans. Inspired by the exotic fabrics and braids she saw as she trailed after her mother in the Damascus *suq*, or that were secreted in her mother's cupboards at home, Thea went on to create the beautiful garments featured in this book. That memory also informed the way she dressed herself, and the forms in which she decorated the places where she lived and worked. It also found perfect harmony with the French Romantic literature Thea grew to love, in particular the evocation of eastern luxury in the poems of Charles Baudelaire. A favourite was *L'invitation au voyage*: Baudelaire's words alone ('Les riches plafonds, / Les miroirs profonds, / La splendeur orientale ... ')[7] are the perfect description of the mirrored table and walls where Thea's legendary dinner parties took place. But most of all it was the writing of Marcel Proust (1871–1922) she loved for the way in which he described garments and fabrics:

He understood that the clothes women wear are pointers to their character. With the eye of a painter or a dress designer, Proust wrote eloquently of clothes and of combinations of colours and fabrics – of lilac and cream, purple and black, of striped and moired silk, of soft heavy negligés draped over powdered arms. When he writes of a frothy, lacy blouse, one is reminded of a Renoir or a Frith; when he details a street costume – a Rembrandt hat, a skunk coat and a bunch of violets – a Vuillard comes to mind; and when he describes a woman wearing layers of black velvet over white faille with orchids in her hair, it is as if one were in front of a portrait by Whistler. Perhaps painters and dress designers have more in common than is realized.[8]

As a painter herself, Thea's love and use of colour was honed by her artistic practice in Beirut and her deep knowledge of history of art, making her observations on other artists extremely apposite. In her 'scrapbook' she described the French symbolist painter Gustave Moreau (1826–98) as one of her heroes, because: 'Like me, Moreau was greatly influenced by the East – or at least by an imaginary nineteenth century version of the East.'[9] It is most telling, given her later career as a designer and her ability to take an ephemeral idea and turn it into a physical object of beauty, that she also identified with Moreau's view that: 'Art is the strenuous attempt to express inner feeling in plastic form.'[10]

The background to Thea Porter's story and the scope of her achievement as discussed here is truly international, but her narrative is also uniquely bound up with Britain, encapsulating an extraordinary moment in time, with Soho and 'Swinging London' at its heart. As she reflected back on that time she wrote in her memoir:

In this scrapbook, I have tried to recapture some moments of my youth and working life, and some of the dresses I created as my contribution to that volcanic eruption in British life, that frenzied breaking of taboos, known as the Swinging Sixties, but which in fact stretched well into the Seventies. At the time, I was hardly aware that I was part of a revolution. I was too busy working, too immersed in the day-to-day struggle. Now that it's over and long since gone, its fun to look back on.[11]

Venetia Porter

Notes

Introduction

1 de la Haye (ed.) 1997; Koda and Martin 1994 and Whitley 2013
2 February–May 2015.
3 This section, the first part of the chapter Damascus & Beirut and the Afterword are written by Venetia Porter. The other sections are written by Laura McLaws Helms.
4 This material is in the Archive of Art & Design AAD/1995/4.
5 Thea Porter, *Scrapbook*, p.76. There were various versions of Thea Porter's *Scrapbook*. A complete text was edited by Thea's brother Patrick and offered unsuccessfully to various publishers. Here, we refer to this as 'Thea Porter, *Scrapbook*' and it contains 77 pages. This version of the *Scrapbook* will be available online in 2015. All unattributed quotes in the text that follows are taken from this document. Also in the V&A archive, and with Venetia Porter (hereafter 'VP archive'), are pages and notes from earlier drafts and these are referred to as 'Thea Porter, *Scrapbook*, early draft' specifying the location of the document.

Damascus & Beirut

1 The London Society for Promoting Christianity amongst the Jews (also known as the London Jews' Society) was founded in 1809. Morris describes his activities in London and Palestine in 'Some experiences of Jewish work', Missionary Herald (Presbyterian Church of Ireland), August 1933, pp.191–2.
2 She attended an institution called Swanwick in Alfreton, Derbyshire, between 1917 and 1920.
3 His ordination is noted in the Missionary Herald, November 1933, p.265. Morris was the author of *The Desert Bible* (Worthing 1974) and *Qur'an and Bible* (London 1978).
4 Seale 1988, p.14–21
5 See Seale 1965
6 Thea Porter, *Scrapbook*, pp.3–4. At this stage the family were known as Sigel. In about 1948 they changed their name to Seale. Morris would later refer to himself in his publications as Morris S. Seale.
7 Thea Porter, *Scrapbook*, p.4. Dr Sabra, who knew Morris Seale in Beirut, said that he took charge of two churches and an evening school (From an email exchange between Christine Lindner and Venetia Porter, 28 May 2014).
8 Thea Porter, *Scrapbook*, p.5
9 Thea Porter, *Scrapbook*, p.5
10 Thea Porter, *Scrapbook*, p.5
11 Thea Porter, *Scrapbook*, p.1
12 Thea Porter, *Scrapbook*, p.7
13 Thea Porter, *Scrapbook*, p.8
14 Patrick Seale, Eulogy, Memorial Service, 26 October 2000 (VP archive)
15 Fernhill Manor School in New Milton was founded in 1919. After the war it was purchased by Winifred Duplock (who Thea refers to as Dewdrop in her letters) and Mary Hanbidge, and reopened to include boarders and day girls. Thea's sister Barbara, known as Bobbie, had left Syria before the war. She went on to become a marine biologist and married Beecher Moore in 1954. She died in 1971. They had one son Chadwick.
16 Letter from Thea Porter, February 1947 (VP archive)
17 Letter from Thea Porter, 9 March 1947 (VP archive)
18 Letter from Thea Porter, 22 June 1947 (VP archive)
19 Letter from Thea Porter, 18 May 1947 (VP archive)
20 Letter from Thea Porter, 8 June 1947 (VP archive)
21 Undated letter from Thea Porter, presumed Autumn 1947 (VP archive)
22 Letter from Thea Porter, 24 April 1947 (VP archive)
23 Letter from Thea Porter, 24 July 1947 (VP archive)
24 Ibid.
25 Letter from Thea Porter, 30 May 1948 (VP archive)
26 Letter from Thea Porter, 14 November 1948 (VP archive)
27 Letter from Thea Porter, 14 November 1948 (VP archive)
28 Thea Porter, *Scrapbook*, p.9
29 Thea Porter, *Scrapbook*, p.10
30 Kingston 1996, pp.64–5
31 Thea Porter, *Scrapbook*, p.10
32 Traboulsi 2012, p.135 ff
33 Thea Porter, *Scrapbook*, p.13
34 A close friend was May Jumblatt, the estranged wife of the Druze politician Kamal, who was assassinated in 1977. For the latest publication on Kim Philby see Macintyre 2014.
35 Bob Porter was involved in foreign aid to Jordan (see Kingston 1996, p.150). King Hussein awarded him the Order of the Jordanian Star (2nd class).
36 Thea Porter, *Scrapbook*, p.12
37 Bob Porter in conversation with his daughter Venetia Porter.
38 Thea Porter, *Scrapbook*, p.13
39 Thea Porter, *Scrapbook*, p.13
40 Thea Porter, *Scrapbook*, p.13
41 Thea Porter, *Scrapbook*, p.14
42 Notes for 'Thea Porter's *Scrapbook*', (VP archive). The Lebanese Prime Minister was Rachid Karami. See also Traboulsi 2012, pp.138 ff
43 Thea Porter, *Scrapbook*, p.12
44 From an interview by Venetia Porter with Jalal Khoury, July 2012.
45 Thea Porter, *Scrapbook*, p.11; for further details on these artists see Guiragossian 2013; for Aref Rayyes see *Liban – Le Regard des Peintres* 1989, pp.144–5.
46 Fateh al-Moudarres (Paris and Damascus 1995); Khalil Zgheib in Fani 1998, pp.261–4; see also: *Liban – Le Regard des Peintres* 1989, pp.162–3.
47 Thea Porter, *Scrapbook*, p.11
48 For Georges Cyr see Fani 1998, pp.84–7 and *Liban – Le Regard des Peintres* 1989, pp.66–8. For Madame Aubry Beaulieu see Duquette and Vasseur 1982 and artotheque.ca/evenements/exposition-hommage-à-simone-aubry-beaulieu (accessed 15 October 2004)
49 The Alecco Saab gallery was founded by the decorator Alecco Saab and major artists exhibited their work there: Paul Guiragossian, in 1960, Michel Basbous, Helen Khal and others. See also: Rogers 2008, pp.142 ff. A review of the 1961 exhibition was written by Nicole Rubeiz, 'Les toiles de Théa Porter: une étrange volière éblouissante d'humour', *L'Orient Le Jour*, 9 June 1961.
50 Fani 1998, p.217
51 *Al-Usbu' al-'Arabi*, 12 June 1961
52 Thea Porter, *Scrapbook*, p.6
53 *Al-Hayat*, February (6 Shbat) 1963
54 Thea Porter, *Scrapbook*, p.12

Damascus & Beirut: *Design inspiration and the Middle East*

1 Ray Connolly, 'Oh! Mrs Porter!', *Evening Standard*, 23 September 1973
2 The library at Thea Porter's home in Bolton Street was full of books on Middle Eastern fashion, Japanese clothes and Islamic and Western art. She would also spend much time in museums drawing details of clothing. One of her favourite books was François Boucher's *Histoire du costume* (Paris 1965). Comment, VP.
3 Baker 1995. An Eastern influenced piece by the House of Reville is included in de la Haye, Taylor and Thompson 2005, appendix 84; it is part of the collection of the Brighton Museum & Art Gallery (CT004062).
4 Koda and Martin 1994, p.62
5 Thea Porter, 'What are clothes about?, *Scrapbook*, undated early draft, p.9 (V&A archive)
6 Thea Porter, *Scrapbook*, p.73

7   De Osma 1980, p.115

8   The first pleated capes were made by Meg Lake, who recalls how the hem needed to be hand rolled in order to make it fan out (from an interview by Venetia Porter with Meg Lake, 7 June 2014).

9   Marylou Luther, letter to Thea Porter, 27 August 1980, Thea Porter paper archive, AAD/1995/4/11, V&A (accessed 10 August 2010)

10 *Tommy Nutter: Rebel On The Row*, exhibition at the Fashion and Textile Museum, London 2011. See also Gormon 2006, ch. 5; Chenoune and Muller 2010.

11 'YSL Timeline', *New York Times*, 8 January 2002: nytimes. com/2002/01/08/style/08iht-ftime_ed3_.html (accessed 2 March 2014)

12 Whitley 2013. See also Webb 2008; Hulanicki 1983; Rhodes and Knight 1985; Watt 2003.

13 From an interview by Laura McLaws Helms with Janet Taylor, 19 December 2013.

14 Turner 2004

15 Helga De Silva Blow Perera, email to Laura McLaws Helms, 11 January 2014.

16 Poiret 2009, p.178

17 Thea Porter, *Scrapbook*, p.68

18 Thea Porter, *Scrapbook*, pp.41–3; more detail in Thea Porter, 'Eight Key Dresses', in Thea Porter, *Scrapbook*, undated and unnumbered early draft (V&A archive).

19 For more information on the shifts in design and fashion during the 1970s, see Lutyens and Hislop 2009.

20 Anawalt 2007, p.46

21 El Giundi 2004, p.369

22 Christopher Ward, 'Can you tell your *Qumbaz* from your *Djellaba*?', *Daily Mirror*, 10 August 1968. Christopher Ward's wedding suit made by Thea was donated to the V&A.

23 Ibid.

24 Christopher Ward, 'With kaftans, as with kilts, the problem is undies', *Daily Mirror*, 21 January 1967

25 Koda and Martin 1994, p.11

26 On Poiret: Deslandres 1987, p.96. See also Thea Porter, 'The Story of Greek Street', in Thea Porter, *Scrapbook*, undated and unnumbered early draft (V&A archive): 'It is difficult to look chic in a real ethnic kaftan or *djellaba*, but luckily Balenciaga re-cut a man's Moroccan robe and gave it chic.'

27 Patricia McColl, 'Couture Arabesque', *Aramco World Magazine*, March–April 1977, p.32

28 A *thawb* is a woman's ankle-length, long-sleeved robe-like tunic. While it is often heavily embroidered in Palestine, a plain white version is traditional male dress in the Persian Gulf. See Lindisfarne-Tapper and Ingham 1997, p.44.

29 Heather Colyer Ross, 'Fashion in the Sand', *Aramco World Magazine*, November–December 1980, p.9

30 Photographed by Barry Lategan. Uncredited author, 'Turkey: Chameleon Clothes Journey into the Present Past', British *Vogue*, November 1971, p.125

31 Thea Porter, *Scrapbook*, p.42

32 Reported in 1975 to cost $700 a piece, Porter's *abayas* were a luxury product. Her best clients in the early 1970s were artists, creative professionals and the wives of wealthy Middle Eastern clients, who she recalled sometimes spent up to $25,000 in a one-hour spree, buying up to 35 *abayas* at a time. See Marian Christy, 'London Designer Thea Porter is Five-Foot Giant in World of Fashion', *Lakeland Ledger*, 18 September 1975.

33 Rhodes and Knight 1985, p.26

34 Photographed by Clive Arrowsmith. Uncredited author, 'How you dress is an escape and an adventure in itself … even more so in the evening', British *Vogue*, December 1970, p.88

35 Baker 1995, pp.85–105

36 Jullian 1977, p.28 ff (Delacroix); p.48 ff (Géricault)

37 Photographed by David Bailey. Uncredited author, 'Prettiest evening looks', British *Vogue*, February 1969

38 Ribeiro 2004, p.49

39 Hana Chidiac, wall text in *L'Orient des Femmes vu par Christian Lacroix* exhibition, Musée du Quai Branly, Paris 2011

40 Thea Porter, undated and unlabelled note (V&A archive). A similarly panelled gown with scalloped edges from Entari in Turkey dates from c.1900 (fig. 19, V&A: T.96-1954).

41 Thea Porter, *Scrapbook*, pp.42–3

42 Anawalt 2007, p.101

43 Anawalt 2007, pp.101, 117

44 From an interview by Laura McLaws Helms with Julian Yearwood, 28 June 2014.

45 From an interview by Venetia Porter with Meg Lake, 7 June 2014.

46 Goncharova designed costumes and stage sets for several of the Ballets Russes from 1914. Her work was known for exhibiting an 'intellectual interest in the handicrafts and rituals of Old Russia,' which was incorporated into her costume design. See Jane Pritchard, 'The Transformation of Ballet' in Pritchard 2010, p.49; and John E. Bowlt, 'Léon Bakst, Natalia Goncharova and Pablo Picasso', also in Pritchard 2010, p.107.

47 Thea Porter, *Scrapbook*, p.71

48 Thea Porter, 'Eight Key Dresses', in Thea Porter, *Scrapbook*, undated and unnumbered early draft (V&A archive)

49 The dress was shown in the V&A exhibition *The Wedding Dress: 500 Years of Bridal Fashion* (2014).

50 Thea Porter, 'Eight Key Dresses', in Thea Porter, *Scrapbook*, undated and unnumbered early draft (V&A archive)

51 Uncredited author, 'The New Theo-Logians', *Women's Wear Daily*, 22 June 1971

52 Thea Porter, *Scrapbook*, p.43

53 From an interview by Laura McLaws Helms with Jan de Villeneuve, 24 September 2013.

54 Thea Porter, 'Eight Key Dresses', in Thea Porter, *Scrapbook*, undated and unnumbered (V&A archive). The Chazaras were made by Mrs Pall.

55 Antique braids were brought regularly to the shop by a Mr Taliaken, and Meg Lake recalls the great excitement when he arrived with his little suitcase full of them, as they never knew what he would bring; interview by Venetia Porter with Meg Lake, 7 June 2014.

56 Thea Porter, *Scrapbook*, p.41

57 Also known as *sarwal*. See Lindisfarne-Tapper and Ingham 1997, p.44 and elsewhere.

58 See for example *Odalisque in Red Trousers* by Henri Matisse in Jullian 1977, p.179; Thea Porter, *Scrapbook*, p.43.

59 Amy de la Haye, 'Ethnic Minimalism: A strand of 1990s British Identity explored via contextual analysis of designs by Shirin Guild', in White and Griffiths 2000.

60 Photographed by Barry Lategan. Uncredited author, 'Never Before Coats', British *Vogue*, November 1970, p.116

61 These rugs are known as *Samawa* after the place in which they were made. Gillow 2010, p.118.

62 Whitley 2013, pp.104–5

London 1964–1974

1   Ann Barr, 'Thea Porter: When Middle Eastern fashion came to London', *The Guardian*, 26 July 2000

2   Marian Christy, 'London Designer Thea Porter is Five-Foot Giant in World of Fashion', *Lakeland Ledger*, 18 September 1975: 'Most talked-about job was one wing of the Syrian embassy which she turned into a splendid blur of Persian prints, Persian rugs and Middle Eastern furniture inlaid with mother of pearl designs.'

3   Barbara Ann Taylor, 'Any bachelor's ideal pad', *Evening Standard*, 15 September 1966, p.8

4   Uncredited author, 'Istanbul Style Boutique: All the Comforts of the Eastern markets', *Scotsman*, 18 December 1965

5 Ibid.

6 Ibid.

7 Ann Barr, 'Passion for Pattern', *House and Garden*, February 1969, p.35

8 Thea Porter, *Scrapbook*, p.18. Peter Kilner (d.2000) met Thea in Beirut where he ran the Arab News Agency. Diana Wordsworth (d. late 1980s) met Thea in London. She was an intrepid traveller and spent much of her life in Rajasthan.

9 Thea Porter, *Scrapbook*, p.18

10 Thea Porter, *Scrapbook*, p.18

11 Thea Porter, 'The Story of Greek Street', in Thea Porter, *Scrapbook*, undated and unnumbered early draft (V&A archive)

12 Piri Halasz, 'London: The Swinging City', *Time Magazine*, 15 April 1966

13 Sonia Ashmore, 'Far Out and Way In: London as Fashion Cosmopolis 1945–1979', in Breward 2006, p.208. See also Whitley 2013.

14 Ashmore in Breward 2006, p.209

15 Christopher Ward, 'With kaftans, as with kilts, the problem is undies', *Daily Mirror*, 21 January 1967. See also Whitley 2013.

16 Thea Porter, *Scrapbook*, p.19

17 Thea Porter, 'The Story of Greek Street', in Thea Porter, *Scrapbook*, undated and unnumbered early draft (V&A archive)

18 Eleni, '"Same Fabric" On All', *Washington Star*, 18 August 1971

19 Thea Porter, *Scrapbook*, p.20

20 From an interview by Laura McLaws Helms with Claudia Bruce Dematio, 25 February 2014.

21 Thea Porter, *Scrapbook*, p.20

22 Thea Porter, 'The Story of Greek Street', in Thea Porter, *Scrapbook*, undated and unnumbered scrap (V&A archive)

23 Thea Porter, *Scrapbook*, p.24

24 From a telephone interview by Laura McLaws Helms with Michael Butler, in which he reminisced about the more than 20 pieces Thea made for him, and recalled being attracted to them for their theatricality and good taste, 15 November 2013.

25 Thea Porter, *Scrapbook*, p.24. Men's suits were made by the tailor Mr Pall in Clifford Street.

26 Thea Porter, *Scrapbook*, p.23

27 Thea dedicated her memoir to Melanie Miller and Marylou Luther. Thea Porter, *Scrapbook*, early draft (VP archive).

28 Thea Porter, *Scrapbook*, p.25

29 Bernadine Morris, 'Fashions Design with Nostalgic Look', *New York Times*, 12 October 1970

30 Bonny Spencer, 'Thea Porter', *Ritz*, October 1981, p.45

31 Thea Porter, *Scrapbook*, p.70

32 From a telephone interview by Laura McLaws Helms with Louise Fennell, 2 April 2011.

33 A more in-depth analysis of outworkers and small factories within the British fashion system can be found in McRobbie 1998.

34 From a telephone interview by Laura McLaws Helms with Louise Fennell, 2 April 2011.

35 From a telephone interview by Laura McLaws Helms with Carla Codara, 2 April 2011.

36 From a telephone interview by Laura McLaws Helms with Louise Fennell, 2 April 2011.

37 From an interview by Laura McLaws Helms with Venetia Porter, 9 January 2011.

38 Madeliene Corey, 'Some Patterns for Today', *The Providence Journal*, 12 July 1971

39 From an interview by Laura McLaws Helms with Sandra Munro Moscardini, 27 February 2014.

40 Interestingly, a Beardsley retrospective was on display at the V&A Museum in 1966, and proved highly influential on many aspects of British high art and pop culture at the time – the album cover for the Beatles' *Revolver* being a key example. See Nigel Whiteley, 'Pop, Consumerism, and the Design Shift,' *Design Issues*, no. 2 (Autumn 1985), p.41.

41 Thea Porter, *Scrapbook*, p.12

42 Thea Porter, *Scrapbook*, p.46

43 Thea Porter, 'The Story of Greek Street', in Thea Porter, *Scrapbook*, undated early draft, p.4 (V&A archive)

44 Thea Porter, *Scrapbook*, p.23; Jimi Hendrix ordered one of these.

45 The fabric is incorrectly called a 'Persian silk', but is Sandra Munro's Peacock print. Bill Cunningham, 'Mystery of the Middle East', *Chicago Tribune*, 21 June 1971.

46 Uncredited author, 'Cecil Beaton's own gallery of fashion', British *Vogue*, October 1971, p.121. Beaton 1971.

47 Thea Porter, 'Raw Materials: Fabrics', in Thea Porter, *Scrapbook*, undated early draft, p.8 (V&A archive)

48 Rhodes and Knight 1985, pp.91–4

49 The authors have been unable to locate Sheila Hudson.

50 Thea Porter, 'Raw Materials: Fabrics', in Thea Porter, *Scrapbook*, undated early draft, p.1 (V&A archive)

51 The authors have been unable to locate Hannah Meckler.

52 Anawalt 2007, p.597

53 Thea Porter, 'Raw Materials: Fabrics', in Thea Porter, *Scrapbook*, undated early draft, p.8 (V&A archive)

54 Patrick married Lamorna Heath in 1972; she died in 1978. They had two children, Orlando and Delilah. He subsequently married Rana Kabbani in 1985 and they had two children, Yasmine and Alexander.

55 Uncredited author, 'Patterns of Persian Living: Michael Szell in Iran, S.W.7 ... Thea Porter too', British *Vogue*, July 1971, p.122. Thea Porter and Michael Szell's collaboration was described as a 'fusion of two talents, both pushing originality in design for wearing as well as for home decoration' (see *Daily Express*, 21 July 1971)

56 See Porter 1995, p.66 and p.117, for examples of Persian and Syrian tiles with floral and arabesque motifs of the type that Szell abstracted and amplified in his textile designs. The paisley design derives from a flowering plant motif known as *buta*. See also Baker 1995, p.129.

57 Jutta was married to Scottish psychiatrist R.D. Laing, author of numerous books including *The Divided Self: An Existential Study in Sanity and Madness* (London 1960) and *Knots* (London 1970).

58 Thea Porter, 'Eight Key Dresses', Thea Porter, *Scrapbook*, undated and unnumbered early draft (V&A archive)

59 From an interview by Laura McLaws Helms with Venetia Porter, 9 January 2011.

60 Thea Porter, 'History', undated draft, p.2 (V&A archive)

61 Uncredited author, 'Two designers who feel they make "beautiful clothes"...', *Draper's Record*, 9 December 1972, p.32

62 Joan Juliet Buck, 'The Princess and the Theas', *Women's Wear Daily*, 27 September 1973

63 Thea Porter, *Scrapbook*, p.32

64 From an interview by Laura McLaws Helms with Lady Annabel Goldsmith, 25 September 2013.

65 Correspondence between Baroness Rawlings and Venetia Porter, 22 September 2014.

66 Anne Price, 'The Romantic Look of London', *Country Life*, 19 March 1970, p.725

67 Thea Porter, *Scrapbook*, p.20

68 Felicity Green, 'April Ashley on Clothes', *Daily Mirror*, 16 March 1970, p.15

69 From an interview by Laura McLaws Helms with Marylou Luther, 2 December 2013.

70 Marylou Luther, 'Price Tag Put on Rich Hippie Game', *Los Angeles Times*, 29 March 1970, D12

71 Thea Porter, *Scrapbook*, early draft (VP archive). Harun al-Rashid (r.789–809) was one of the most famous caliphs of the Muslim world, with his capital in Baghdad. In her memoir, Porter wrote: 'Madame Kamal Adham, is a dazzling Turkish lady of great breeding, with huge eyes, high cheekbones and the whitest of white skins – a beauty almost as mesmerising as Elizabeth

It was both fun and flattering that she chose her jewellery and her furs to match my clothes rather than the other way round. I sensed what dresses she would like and had fabrics made especially for her. On one occasion when she was unwell, her husband, a large commanding figure, came to the shop himself and carried off an armful of kaftans to cheer her up.' Thea Porter, *Scrapbook*, p.45.

72 These included Maryam and Fereshte Massoudi.

73 Photographed by Henry Clarke. Uncredited author, 'Porter's Museum-Piece Velvets', British *Vogue*, December 1969

74 Anne Price, 'The Romantic Look of London', *Country Life*, 19 March 1970, p.724

75 Thea Porter, *Scrapbook*, p.19. See also Parkin 2012; there are several references to Thea throughout the book, including a photograph by Patrick Lichfield on p.117.

76 Ann Barr, 'Passion for Pattern', *House and Garden*, February 1969, p.36. The Bolton Street flat had originally belonged to her friend and co-founder of the Greek Street shop, Diana Wordsworth.

77 Author unknown, '…in a mirror wall', unmarked and undated newspaper clipping (VP archive)

78 Ibid. The mirrored dining room is also featured in Skurka 1972.

79 Thea Porter, 'A Selfish Sunday in London', *Telegraph*, March 1977

80 Ibid.

81 From correspondence between Fran Yorke (then Barker) and Venetia Porter, 1 July 2014.

82 Thea Porter, *Scrapbook*, p.34. See also *Daily Express*, 1971 (undated but sometime in the final week of June). Among the employees of the 1970s and early 1980s were also Di Follett and Jonty Scott.

83 From correspondence between Venetia Porter and Louise Fennell, 8 May 2014.

84 From an interview by Laura McLaws Helms with Jan de Villeneuve, 24 September 2013.

85 Thea Porter, *Scrapbook*, p.40

86 In 1974, Prudence Glyn also attended Modfest and wrote 'Britain's Thea Porter and Bill Gibb were both in fine form. Both have shown at Modfest before and both confess that it was partially the loveliness of the place and the fun of the occasion that brought them back'. *The Times*, 13 August 1974.

87 A booklet containing short biographies of the designers accompanied the show. Of those included, only Zandra Rhodes and Jean Muir continued to have highly successful fashion design careers into the 1980s and 1990s, although Mary Quant remained the head of a fashion and cosmetics empire until 2000.

New York 1968–1971

1 Thea Porter, *Scrapbook*, p.25

2 Jane Holzer described her Thea Porter clothes as: 'like wearing a *king's* raiment … they're so *splendid*.' Uncredited author, 'Everybody's Talking…', American *Vogue*, 15 November 1968.

3 Jo-An Jenkins, 'Bendel's Porter', *Women's Wear Daily*, 3 November 1969

4 Phyllis Feldkamp, untitled article, *Philadelphia Bulletin*, 1970

5 Thea Porter, *Scrapbook*, p.47

6 Fabian and Byrne 2005, p.10

7 'I was playing pool at Giorgio's the other day, and I saw two gals come in together…. By the time they'd left … each of those two ragamuffins had bought three dresses, a Chloé, a Thea Porter, and a Zandra Rhodes – not one of them much less than two thousand dollars.' Krantz 1978, pp.254, 264.

8 Press Release for Eleanor Lambert Inc., 'Thea Porter: For Immediate Release', 18 May 1971

9 Ibid.

10 David Curry, 'A beautiful way to spend money', *Financial Times*, 18 May 1971

11 Press Release for Eleanor Lambert Inc., 'Thea Porter: For Immediate Release', 18 May 1971

12 A photograph of Boo wearing a Thea Porter dress is featured in *Andy Warhol* (exhib. cat., Moderna Museet Stockholm, 1968), no page numbers.

13 Press Release for Eleanor Lambert Inc., 'Thea Porter: For Immediate Release', 18 May 1971

14 Jody Jacobson, 'Porter-House Stake', *Women's Wear Daily*, 1971

15 Thea Porter, *Scrapbook*, p.51

16 Frank Drake, 'Playboy's collection', *Cleveland Press*, 27 December 1971

17 Aquilina Ross 2011, p.79.

18 David Curry, 'A beautiful way to spend money', *Financial Times*, 18 May 1971

19 Thea Porter, *Scrapbook*, pp.52–3

Los Angeles 1969–1979

1 Thea Porter, *Scrapbook*, p.53

2 Thea Porter, *Scrapbook*, p53

3 From an interview by Laura McLaws Helms with Linda Dresner, 6 October 2013.

4 Yvonne Petrie, 'Thea Porter', *Detroit News*, 21 May 1974

5 Thea Porter, 'The Story of Greek Street', in Thea Porter, *Scrapbook*, undated early draft (V&A archive).

6 Haber 1976, p.190

7 Anthony Burton, 'People', *Daily News*, 11 June 1975

8 Rita Palmer, 'I Only Believe in Beauty', *Newsweek*, 29 August 1977, p.48

9 From an interview by Laura McLaws Helms with Veronique Peck, 2 September 2011.

10 Ibid.

11 Thea Porter, *Scrapbook*, undated and unnumbered early draft (V&A archive)

12 Thea Porter, *Scrapbook*, p.44

13 Ibid.

14 Ibid.

15 Rita Palmer, 'I Only Believe in Beauty', *Newsweek*, 29 August 1977, p.48

16 From a telephone interview by Laura McLaws Helms with Fred Hayman, 8 April 2013.

17 Ibid.

18 From a telephone interview by Laura McLaws Helms with Lorna Luft, 1 November 2013.

19 Thea Porter, *Scrapbook*, p.57

20 Thea Porter, letter to Veronique Peck, 31 May 1979 (V&A archive)

21 Harriet Shapiro, 'One thing that makes the rich different is that they can afford Thea Porter's caftans', *People*, 9 January 1978, p.71

22 Ibid.

23 Ibid.

24 From an interview by Laura McLaws Helms with Crystal Gayle, 13 August 2013.

25 Raina Grossan, 'How stars dress: Porter gives tips', *Argus-Press*, 9 August 1980

26 From an interview by Laura McLaws Helms with Crystal Gayle, 13 August 2013.

27 From an interview by Laura McLaws Helms with Jonty Scott, 3 March 2014.

28 From a telephone interview by Laura McLaws Helms with Fiona Dunlop, 7 March 2014.

Paris 1971–1979

1 Thea Porter, *Scrapbook*, p.21

2 Thea Porter, 'History', undated and unnumbered (V&A archive)

3 From a telephone interview by Laura McLaws Helms with Katharine Hamnett, 20 January 2014.

4 Jody Jacobson, 'Porter-House Stake', *Women's Wear Daily*, 1971

5 Thea Porter, *Scrapbook*, p.57

6 Comment, VP.

7 Thea Porter, *Scrapbook*, p.58

8 Ray Connolly, 'Oh! Mrs Porter!', *Evening Standard,* 23 September 1973

9 Thea Porter, *Scrapbook*, p.59

10 Bernadine Morris, 'The Fall Game: Peasants and Indians', *New York Times Magazine*, 9 May 1976, p.191

11 Marylou Luther, 'Thea Porter Puts On a Good Front', *Los Angeles Times*, 22 May 1977, H1

12 Marian Christy, 'She's riding crest of the present craze', *Boston Sunday Globe*, 26 December 1976

13 'Notes on Proposal for Introduction of Additional Capital and Appointment of Directors [for Thea Porter Decorations Ltd.]', June 1968 (V&A Archive)

14 From an interview by Laura McLaws Helms with Venetia Porter, 9 January 2011.

15 From a telephone interview by Laura McLaws Helms with Fiona Dunlop, 7 March 2014.

16 Sarah Drummond, 'High-Powered People', *Harpers & Queen*, January 1978

17 From a telephone interview by Laura McLaws Helms with Fiona Dunlop, 7 March 2014.

18 Thea Porter, 'History', undated, p.3 (V&A archive)

19 From an interview by Laura McLaws Helms with Louise Fennell, 29 September 2011.

20 Thea Porter, *Scrapbook*, p.60

21 Thea Porter, 'Disasters', in Thea Porter, *Scrapbook*, undated and unnumbered early draft (V&A archive)

22 Antoine was one of the directors of Thea Porter Decorations Ltd during the late 1970s. At one stage he did briefly take on managerial responsibilities.

23 Thea Porter, 'History', undated, p.3 (V&A archive)

24 'Proposal for Marketing Thea Porter Products', 1979 (V&A archive)

25 'Agreement for the establishment of an enterprise to exploit certain designs and products under the name and marks "THEA PORTER"', 19 July 1979 (V&A Archive)

26 Peter Salmon had been the finance director and strategic advisor of the companies that had merchandized and greatly expanded the businesses of Mary Quant, with her full involvement, artistic control and consequent financial reward. He had also rescued the old clothes label firm Tinsley Robor and so had experience of the less glamorous side of the textile industry. He was a client of Chenciner and they had arranged previous deals together, and Chenciner introduced him and his proposal to Porter. Thea was a good friend, who in 1978, had generously lent one of her shimmering red gowns to Chenciner for the legendary prima ballerina Svetlana Beriosova to wear in his film of his ballet *Steps Notes and Squeaks*, devised by Maina Gielgud. Chenciner felt that her fears were based on misunderstanding and regretted that the deal never came through. From an interview by Venetia Porter with Robert Chenciner, 9 July 2014.

27 From an interview by Laura McLaws Helms with Jonty Scott, 3 March 2014.

London 1976–1989

1 A *yashmak* (also known as a *niqab*) is a face veil, worn by some Muslim women, that covers the entire face except for the eyes. See Lindisfarne-Tapper and Ingham 1997, p.45; and 'Capital Clothes', *Harper's & Queen*, March 1977, p.140.

2 Anne-Marie Schiro, 'International Style', *New York Times*, 3 October 1976

3 Bernadine Morris, 'Spring Collections at a Leisurely Pace', *New York Times*, 22 November 1977, p.58

4 From an interview by Laura McLaws Helms with Louise Fennell, September 2011.

5 Thea Porter, *Scrapbook*, p.60

6 Thea Porter, 'History of Thea Porter Decorations Ltd.', undated (V&A archive)

7 From an interview by Laura McLaws Helms with Louise Fennell, September 2011.

8 Frances Gibb, 'Top fashion designers to go out of business', *The Times*, 5 February 1981

9 Ibid.

10 Thea Porter, *Scrapbook*, p.60

11 Bernadine Morris, 'In Britain, a Week of Fashion', *New York Times*, 16 October 1981, B4

12 Thea Porter, *Scrapbook*, p.29

13 Thea Porter, *Scrapbook*, undated and unnumbered early draft (V&A Archive)

14 From an interview by Laura McLaws Helms with Venetia Porter, 9 January 2011.

15 Ruzzini's possessions were listed as including: 'A slashed red jacket lined in felt, and a matching felt-lined cloak, red doublet. A doublet of white fustian, peacock-trimmed cape, a black wool cloak and a plain black wool mantle. A short black skirt (to be worn over tights) underpants, a pair of red shoes and a pair of black shoes, bag of cloves, a breadknife, a bedcover and two embroidered cushions.' Thea Porter, *Scrapbook*, p.77.

16 Other loyal friends at this time included art dealer Henry Elwell, Ann Barr and Jutta Laing. Ann Barr's family donated a collection of 11 Thea Porter garments to the London College of Fashion Special Collections in 2012.

17 She was cared for at Delves House in Queensgate Terrace and died on 24 July 2000 from a chest infection at Chelsea and Westminster Hospital, London.

18 *Tonight*, 21 October 1975 (as broadcast by the BBC from 1975–9)

19 *The Times*, 25 May 1978. Honor Frost sent Thea the cutting and noted: 'Dearest Thea, Your jacket is extremely photogenic!' Interviews by Venetia Porter with B Larsson, Honor Frost (d.2010) and Hanan al-Shaykh.

20 From an interview by Laura McLaws Helms with Andrew Logan, 1 October 2013.

21 Molly Parkin, 'Thea spreads her wings', *Sunday Times*, March 1971

Afterword

1 'Everything passes, everything wears out, everything breaks'. The gravestone is in the rose garden of Kensal Rise cemetery and was carved by Alec Peever.

2 Patrick Seale, who died in 2014, continued to write until the year before his death. In 2010, at the age of 79, he completed the third of his trilogy of books on the Middle East: *The Struggle for Arab Independence Riad el-Solh and the Makers of the Modern Middle East* (Cambridge 2010) and he continued to write articles in Al-Hayat newspaper until 2013. See also: Seale's obituary by Tim Llewellyn, theguardian.com/media/2014/apr/13/patrick-seale, *Guardian* (13 April 2014).

3 Thea Porter, *Scrapbook*, p.1

4 Thea Porter, *Scrapbook*, p.12

5 Thea Porter, *Scrapbook*, p.75: 'I believe in the primacy of the face. Of course a dress must make one aware of the body underneath, either blatantly revealed or skillfully disguised, but even in designing a mini it is important to remember that the face is as important as the legs.'

6 Thea Porter, *Scrapbook*, p.36

7 'The richly-painted ceilings, the fathomless mirrors, the splendor of the East...' Francis Scarfe (ed.), *Baudelaire* (Penguin 1961), p.108. His poem was read out at Thea's memorial service in October 2000.

8 Thea Porter, *Scrapbook*, pp.9–10

9 Thea Porter, *Scrapbook*, p.5

10 Thea Porter, *Scrapbook*, p.68

11 Thea Porter, *Scrapbook*, p.2

Bibliography

Anawalt 2007
Patricia R. Anawalt, *The Worldwide History of Dress* (London 2007)

Aquilina Ross 2011
Geoffrey Aquilina Ross, *The Day of the Peacock* (London 2011)

Baker 1995
Patricia L. Baker, *Islamic Textiles* (London 1995)

Beaton 1971
Cecil Beaton, *Fashion: An Anthology* (London 1971)

Breward 2006
Christopher Breward (ed.), *Fashion's World Cities* (Oxford 2006)

Chenoune and Muller 2010
Florence Chenoune and Farid Muller, *Yves Saint Laurent* (New York 2010)

de la Haye 1997
Amy de la Haye (ed.), *The Cutting Edge* (London 1997)

de la Haye, Taylor and Thompson 2005
Amy de la Haye, Lou Taylor and Eleanor Thompson, *A Family of Fashion: The Messel Dress Collection* (London 2005)

de Osma 1980
Guillermo de Osma, *Mariano Fortuny: His Life and Work* (New York 1980)

Deslandres 1987
Yvonne Deslandres, *Poiret: Paul Poiret 1879–1914* (New York 1987)

Duquette and Vasseur 1982
Jean Pierre Duquette and Annie Molin Vasseur (eds), *Simone Aubry Beaulieu* (Montreal 1982)

El Giundi 2004
Fadwa El Giundi, 'Djellaba', *Encyclopedia of Clothing and Fashion* (New York 2004)

Fabian and Byrne 2005
Jenny Fabian and Johnny Byrne, *Groupie* (London 1969; reprinted London 2005)

Fani 1998
Michel Fani, *Dictionnaire de la peinture au Liban* (Saint Didier 1998)

Gillow 2010
John Gillow, *Textiles of the Islamic World* (New York 2010)

Gormon 2006
Paul Gormon, *The Look* (London 2006)

Guiragossian 2013
Paul Guiragossian, *The Human Condition* (The Paul Guiragossian Foundation and Beirut Art Centre 2013)

Haber 1976
Joyce Haber, *The Users* (New York 1976)

Hulanicki 1983
Barbara Hulanicki, *From A to Biba* (London 1983)

Jullian 1977
Philippe Jullian, *The Orientalists* (Oxford 1977)

Kingston 1996
Paul W.T. Kingston, *Britain and the politics of modernization in the Middle-East 1945–1958* (Cambridge 1996)

Koda and Martin 1994
Harold Koda and Richard Martin, *Orientalism: Visions of the East in Western Dress* (New York 1994)

Krantz 1978
Judith Krantz, *Scruples* (New York 1978)

Liban – Le Regard des Peintres 1989
Liban – Le Regard des Peintres (Barbican Centre, London; Institut du Monde Arabe, Paris, exhib. cat., 1989)

Lindisfarne-Tapper and Ingham 1997
Nancy Lindisfarne-Tapper and Bruce Ingham, *Languages of Dress in the Middle East* (London 1997)

Lutyens and Hislop 2009
Dominic Lutyens and Kirsty Hislop, *'70s Style & Design* (London 2009)

Macintyre 2014
Ben Macintyre, *A Spy Among Friends* (London 2014)

McRobbie 1998
Angela McRobbie, *British Fashion Design: Rag Trade or Image Industry?* (London 1998)

Parkin 2012
Sophie Parkin, *The Colony Room Club 1948–2008* (London 2012)

Poiret 2009
Paul Poiret, *King of Fashion: The Autobiography of Paul Poiret* (reprinted London 2009)

Porter 1995
Venetia Porter, *Islamic Tiles* (London 1995)

Pritchard 2010
Jane Pritchard (ed.), *Diaghilev and the Golden Age of the Ballets Russes 1909–1929* (London 2010)

Rhodes and Knight 1985
Zandra Rhodes and Anne Knight, *The Art of Zandra Rhodes* (Boston 1985)

Ribeiro 2004
Aileen Ribeiro, *Dress and Morality* (Oxford 2004)

Rogers 2008
Sarah A. Rogers, *Postwar art and historical roots of Beirut's cosmopolitanism*, PhD (Massachusetts Institute of Technology 2008)

Seale 1965
Patrick Seale, *The Struggle for Syria* (London 1965)

Seale 1988
Patrick Seale, *Asad: The Struggle for the Middle East* (London 1988)

Skurka 1972
Norma Skurka, *Underground Interiors* (Chicago 1972)

Traboulsi 2012
Fawwaz Traboulsi, *A History of Modern Lebanon* (London 2012)

Turner 2004
Alwyn W. Turner, *The Biba Experience* (Woodbridge 2004)

Watt 2003
Judith Watt, *Ossie Clark, 1965–1974* (London 2003)

Webb 2008
Iain R. Webb, *Bill Gibb: Fashion and Fantasy* (London 2008)

White and Griffiths 2000
Nicola White and Ian Griffiths (eds), *The Fashion Business: Theory Practice, Image* (New York 2000)

Whitley 2013
Lauren Whitley, *Hippie Chic* (Boston 2013)

Acknowledgements

The authors would like to thank the following, who have been interviewed, or provided information and assistance in any number of ways. We would particularly like to thank V&A Publishing for all their care in the production of this book: Zara Anvari, Davina Cheung, Clare Davis, Mark Eastment and Tom Windross. We are also grateful to the book's designer Myfanwy Vernon-Hunt and copy-editor, Rebeka Cohen.

Valerie Adams; Clive Arrowsmith; Caroline Baker; Sophie Baker; Saleh Barakat; Nadine Begdache; Jacqueline Bullen; Claudia Bruce Dimatio; Michael Butler; Sarah Chatto; Amanda Charchian; Robert Chenciner; Carla Codara; Oriole Cullen; Richard Davis; Amy de la Haye; Helga Desilva Blow Perera; Barbaralee Diamonstein-Spielvogel; Linda Dresner; Fiona Dunlop; Britt Ekland; Waddah Faris; Cherie Federau; Louise Fennell; Fenella Fielding; Shirlee Fonda; Madeline Gallay; Crystal Gayle; Lady Annabel Goldsmith; Robin Hambro; Katherine Hamnett; Fred Hayman; Leila Heller; Robert and Tru Helms; Jane Holzer; Kimme Jackson; Celia Joicey; Grace Kenny; Jalal Khouri; Daphne Kilner; Jutta Laing; Meg Lake; B Larsson; Barry Lategan; Lauren Lepire; Christine Lindner; Andrew Logan; Lorna Luft; Marylou Luther; Maryam and Fereshte Massoudi; Sarah Moorehead; Bruno Mossa; Sandra Munro Moscardini; Dennis Nothdruft; Empress Farah Pahlavi; Van Pariser; Charlotte Parry Crooke; Veronique and Cecilia Peck; Elsa Peretti; Baroness Rawlings; Sandy Schreier; Jonty Scott; Yasmine Seale; Nadim Shehadi; Penny Slinger; Kerry Taylor; Janet Taylor; Penelope Tree; Charles, Emily and Rhiannon Tripp; Jan de Villeneuve; Christopher Ward; Julian Yearwood; Kohle Yohannan and Fran Yorke.

Picture Credits

All images © Victoria and Albert Museum, London except:

Courtesy of the Venetia Porter collection /
Image © V&A Photographic Studio: pages 11, 12, 13, 14, 15, 17, 18, 19, 20, 21, 22, 24, 26, 27, 32 (left), 45, 55 (above left), 58 (right), 62, 64, 65, 67, 68, 71 (right), 72, 73, 78 (above right, below right), 81, 84 (right), 85, 86 (left), 90 (right), 92, 95, 100, 101, 102, 110, 116, 126, 133, 140, 141, 143, 144, 146, 150

Clive Arrowsmith / Vogue © Condé Nast Publications Ltd: cover

Aubrey Powell / Hipgnosis / Venetia Porter collection: page 2

Barry Lategan / Vogue © Condé Nast Publications Ltd: page 23, above

Courtesy of the Agial Gallery: page 25

Barry Lategan / Vogue © Condé Nast Publications Ltd: page 32

Design © Steve Thomas: page 33

© Les Editions Jalou « *L'Officiel*, 1976»: page 35

Barry Lategan / Vogue © Condé Nast Publications Ltd: page 37

© Christie's Images Ltd: page 38

Clive Arrowsmith / Vogue © Condé Nast Publications Ltd: page 40

Courtesy of the Fashion Institute of Technology / SUNY, Gladys Marcus Library Department of Special Collections: page 41

© Ron Galella / WireImage / Getty Images: page 46

Courtesy of Country Life, IPC Media: page 55 (below right)

Barry Lategan / Vogue © Condé Nast Publications Ltd: page 61

Arnaud de Rosnay / Vogue © Condé Nast Publications Ltd: page 66

William Lovelace / Stringer / Express / Getty Images: page 67

Cecil Beaton / Vogue © Condé Nast Publications Ltd: page 78

© PA.: page 82, right

© REX / Moviestore Collection: page 83, left

Courtesy of Country Life, IPC Media: page 86, right

© Kerry Taylor Auctions Ltd: page 87

Clive Arrowsmith / Vogue © Condé Nast Publications Ltd: page 89

Courtesy of Empress Farah Pahlavi: page 93 (left)

Henry Clarke / Vogue © Condé Nast Publications Ltd: page 93 (right)

Courtesy of Oberto Gili: page 94

Courtesy of Country Life, IPC Media: page 99

Hogenboom / Vogue © Condé Nast Publications Ltd: page 104

Guy Bourdin / Vogue © Condé Nast Publications Ltd: page 105

Jack Robinson / Vogue © Condé Nast Publications Ltd: page 109

© REX/Courtesy Everett Collection: page 119

© David Steen / Scope Features: page 121

© CBS Photo Archive / Getty Images: page 123

© Les Editions Jalou « *L'Officiel*, 1976»: page 127

© Norman Parkinson Ltd / Courtesy Norman Parkinson Archive: page 135

© ROGER HUTCHINGS / CAMERA PRESS LONDON: page 145

© Courtesy of Hanan al-Shaykh: page 146

Index